Embrace Your True Self: The Shadow Work Book

A Beginner's Guide to Healing Your Inner Child, Deepening Self-Love, and Transforming Your Life With Guided Prompts and Exercises

Maria Sage Starling

Table of Contents

INTRODUCTION 1

RACHEL'S STORY: A TUMULTUOUS LIFE OF DISCONTENTMENT AND DISCONNECTION 3

CHAPTER 1: THE CRUCIAL STARTING POINT FOR TRANSFORMATION: INNER CHILD HEALING 9

MEETING YOUR INNER CHILD AND GETTING TO KNOW THEM BETTER 10
WHY IS INNER CHILD WORK SO IMPORTANT? 12
SIGNS OF AN UNHEALED INNER CHILD 12
THE SOLUTION: SHADOW WORK 14
EMOTIONAL RELEASE EXERCISE 14
Visualization 15
Emotional Release 16
ACKNOWLEDGING THE GIFTS, TALENTS, AND STRENGTHS OF YOUR INNER CHILD 17
Activity: Write a Heartfelt Letter to Your Inner Child 18

CHAPTER 2: THE ROAD TO DEEPENING YOUR SELF-LOVE 21

THE CORE COMPONENTS OF SELF-LOVE 22
HOW YOUR SELF-LOVE IMPACTS ALL YOUR RELATIONSHIPS: THE MIRROR EFFECT 23
HARNESSING SHADOW WORK TO DEEPEN YOUR SELF-LOVE 24
DEEPENING YOUR SELF-LOVE: JOURNALING PROMPTS 24
MIRROR WORK: LEARNING TO SEE AND ACKNOWLEDGE YOUR TRUE REFLECTION 26
GRATITUDE JOURNALING 28

CHAPTER 3: EXPLORING YOUR SHADOW SELF 31

ORIGINS OF SHADOW WORK AND ITS PURPOSE 31
BENEFITS OF DOING SHADOW WORK 33
BUT WHERE DOES THE SHADOW SELF COME FROM? 34
COMMON COMPONENTS OF THE SHADOW SELF 35
BRINGING YOUR SHADOW SELF TO LIGHT 36
30-DAY BRINGING YOUR SHADOW TO LIGHT JOURNALING PROMPTS 36

CHAPTER 4: EFFECTIVELY INTEGRATING YOUR SHADOW SELF INTO YOUR EVERYDAY LIFE 39

WHAT DOES SHADOW INTEGRATION PRACTICALLY MEAN? 40
MORE WAYS TO CONSTRUCTIVELY INTEGRATE YOUR SHADOW 42
EXERCISES FOR CONSTRUCTIVELY INTEGRATING THE SHADOW 43

CHAPTER 5: HARNESSING THE BEAUTY AND POWER OF CREATIVE EXPRESSION HOBBIES AND ACTIVITIES 47

ACTIVITIES AND EXERCISES FOR REVIVING YOUR PLAYFUL SOUL........ 49
THE ROLE YOUR IMAGINATION CAN PLAY IN SHADOW WORK 51

CHAPTER 6: THE MIND-BODY DANCE: SOMATIC AWARENESS 53

USING SOMATIC AWARENESS FOR SHADOW WORK........ 54
WHERE TRAPPED EMOTIONS ARE STORED IN THE BODY 56
HOW TO EFFECTIVELY LISTEN TO YOUR BODY: BODY-SCAN MEDITATION........ 57
HOW TO UNBLOCK SUPPRESSED ENERGY........ 59
RACHEL'S SUCCESSFUL SHADOW WORK JOURNEY THROUGH HARNESSING SOMATIC AWARENESS........ 60

CHAPTER 7: EMBRACING SELF-REFLECTION TO THE CORE........ 65

THE POWER OF SELF-REFLECTION 65
WHY WE RUN AWAY FROM SELF-REFLECTION 68
CONSTRUCTIVE SELF-REFLECTION........ 70
SELF-REFLECTION WEEKLY CHECK-INS: SUGGESTED QUESTIONS TO USE........ 71

CHAPTER 8: GOAL SETTING FOR A STELLAR NEW BEGINNING 75

CREATE A VISION BOARD........ 77
REFLECT ON WHAT YOU DISCOVERED DURING YOUR SHADOW WORK JOURNEY........ 77
Strengths 78
Weaknesses........ 79
Opportunities........ 79
Threats........ 80
SETTING AUTHENTIC AND CLEAR GOALS ALIGNED WITH THE REAL YOU........ 80
HOW TO SET GOALS 81
PREPARING FOR SHADOW-BASED OBSTACLES........ 82
YOUR DAILY LIFE SHOULD BRING YOUR VISION CLOSER TO REALIZATION 83

CHAPTER 9: THRIVING THROUGH RELATIONSHIPS: OPENING YOUR HEART TO OTHERS........ 85

UNDERSTANDING REASONS WHY WE MAY CHOOSE TO LIVE LIKE ISLANDS 86
Self-Preservation 86
Fear........ 87
Emotional Overwhelm 88
Need for Control and Perfection........ 89
Phobias (Social Anxiety)........ 90
WHY WE NEED OTHERS TO HELP US BECOME OUR BEST SELVES........ 91
HOW TO FACE RELATIONSHIP CHALLENGES AND NOT RUN AWAY FROM THEM........ 92

CHAPTER 10: LEVERAGING MINDFULNESS AND GROUNDING TECHNIQUES TO STAY CONNECTED TO YOUR TRUTH 95

The Power of Mindfulness 96
Benefits of Mindfulness 97
Mindfulness and Shadow Work *98*
Grounding Yourself in Your Truth 99
What It Means to Disassociate From the Truth 99
The Role of Your Core Values 100
20 Affirmations for Staying Grounded and Authentic *101*

CONCLUSION 103

ABOUT THE AUTHOR 105

REFERENCES 107

Introduction

Have you ever had a persistent feeling that there's much more to you than who you have been showing up as in your life so far? Or maybe you felt like others see it in you too, that you are greater than what you display on the surface. Sometimes, you might even look at your life and wonder why it seldom reflects the full extent of the greatness you have that you can see and feel within you. The fear of continuing to live with so many unused opportunities and potential or buried dreams starts to mount with time. Eventually, it becomes unbearable; you wonder what it will take for you to just finally become that amazing person you have in your sights. How do we explain all that? What is that phenomenon? You probably guessed it right: *It's your deeper undiscovered potential desperately waiting to be unleashed!*

It's also the cry of the inherent strengths and gifts locked in hidden parts of you that will be demanding that you now take action and embrace them. It's your soul crying out to be set free so it can shine in its full splendor and brilliance.

Sometimes, this cry can come in the form of things constantly going wrong in your personal and professional life, thus demanding you to free your higher self and no longer let the condensed version of you continue to run the show. Sometimes, it hits differently, and maybe it's just a sense of serenity that's missing in your life. This may be due to feeling like there are just so many fragmented and unlived parts of you that you wish you could embrace. If you have been consistently feeling this way, you're definitely not alone. Your heart is probing you in the right direction! It's calling you to awaken to who you truly are and learn how to love every side of you.

You are sensing the cry of your heart longing for you to discover and use the gifts that might be locked in parts of your identity that you avoid. This is good! It means now is the time for you to answer the call of being your higher self by learning how to love and integrate parts of yourself that you may have perceived as wrong or shameful. This is what makes shadow work an exhilarating journey you can look forward to. It's the path and process of learning to accept and love every part of yourself, including the parts you may despise about yourself.

Shadow work entails taking time to explore parts of who you are that you may have pushed aside or even pretended don't exist. This includes getting to understand the spectrum of all your emotions, your unspoken desires and fears, your insecurities, and your weaknesses. What makes the shadow work journey impactful is that you don't approach all those parts of yourself you aren't proud of with disdain or judgment. You don't see yourself as being defective or wrong. Instead, shadow work helps you see things from a different perspective. It helps you recognize that every part of you, whether it's perceived as good or bad, still deserves your understanding and compassion. Learning how to integrate your hidden parts can be your ultimate breakthrough to a new life where you get to meet a higher version of yourself who's more integrated and self-accepting. With self-acceptance comes confidence, joy, fulfillment, and so much more!

Think about it. For all of us, there always seems to dawn a time when we may start to feel disconnected from our true selves. Upon reflecting on our lives, we might start to notice recurring patterns of self-doubt, shame, frustration, the same relationship problems, and the same limitations holding us back. These patterns can spread like wildfire across almost every aspect of our lives, be it professionally or personally. Once we notice that something is wrong, we may find ways to avoid facing our reality, and other times, we find ourselves ready to make a change. If we decide to sweep things under the rug and pretend that we don't notice that something isn't right, life has its way of reminding us that problems are meant to be solved, not dismissed. Often, that reminder comes through one thing we all don't like: pain. The beauty of shadow work is that by choosing to dive deep into that journey, you give yourself the chance to fall in love with yourself even more and become someone greater than you've ever allowed yourself to be before.

Rachel's Story: A Tumultuous Life of Discontentment and Disconnection

Many of us will probably relate very well to Rachel's story. She was a beautiful and talented hardworking professional. She was also a responsible mother and loving wife to her dear husband she cared about so much. When looking at Rachel, anyone who didn't know her well would most likely feel like she was probably one of the lucky ladies who lived the "happily ever after" dream. Nevertheless, beneath that exterior, Rachel grew up constantly feeling disconnected not only from others but from herself too. She felt misunderstood and would find herself in disheartening cycles of either one-sided or outright unhealthy relationships. There was undeniable love in her marriage, but she still felt like she was always hitting a wall and unable to forge truly deep connections that reflected the true essence of the person she was. Due to her struggle of failing to accept parts of herself, she judged harshly. She also inadvertently pushed away love sometimes because she felt undeserving and constantly questioned her worth. No matter how much her loving husband tried to reassure her, something inside her would make her feel unlovable at times. This made things very hard for her husband. Rachel's insecurities were evidently taking a toll on their connection.

What made things even more difficult was the fact that as her children grew, they too started to show signs of the same insecurities she had which stemmed from her unhealed or unloved parts. Seeing how she treats herself being reflected back to her through the behavior of her children broke her heart even more. At work, things were also awkward and uncomfortable because it seemed like people would use her insecurities against her and simply start to disrespect her after sensing her insecurities. Thankfully, watching her children struggle was what lit an unquenchable fire in her. Even though previously she didn't have enough courage to fight for herself when it was just her, her love for her children made her even stronger. She was ready to fight this battle with herself and do whatever it took to not allow her children to continue down the same road she knew she loathed being on—a road of self-denial. She thought to herself, "If I can't love all of me for who I truly am, then how can I expect others to do so?"

At first, Rachel couldn't put a finger on what was wrong. She just knew something wasn't right and she had to work on herself, but she didn't comprehend what all her experiences were trying to teach her. It was only much later that she realized that the disconnection she felt for years, the struggle to fully accept and love herself, was all a byproduct of her unhealed wounds from her childhood which troubled her soul all this time. But why didn't she know? It may seem like an obvious thing to figure out easily, but for Rachel, things weren't that simple. She had adapted to life by managing to achieve so much by learning how to suppress parts of herself that she believed herself to be undesirable to others. She trained herself to appear like Superwoman, but deep within, Rachel was just a little girl dearly longing for the freedom to just be vulnerable, receive love, trust others to have her back, and be validated. She was scared of being abandoned to the point of making sure that she would try her best to never allow anyone to see the parts of her she was ashamed of or that she thought people might reject her for. She told herself that those parts dare not be seen by anyone, not even her husband; especially him! She was more afraid to lose him than anyone else. But sadly, her trying to avoid abandonment that way only made it inevitable. She pushed him away by not allowing him to see her for who she truly was inside-out. She sabotaged the intimate bond they could have had just by choosing to only mostly show the parts of her she considered glamorous.

It was through engaging deep in shadow work that Rachel had a lifechanging epiphany. She realized that her life experiences were just reflecting how she was treating herself. Even though it seemed like it was people deliberately hurting her, all that reality was just an outcome of the law of cause and effect. She learned that rejecting or despising parts of herself subconsciously invited other people to also treat her the same. They would also reject and despise the exact things she didn't accept or love about herself. That's the moment she discovered how much power she actually had to change things for the better. Since life was just a mirror of how she was treating herself, she knew that the key to unlocking a different life of true happiness and fulfillment was all up to her. It wasn't other people she had to wait for to change and treat her better. She learned that everything was in her control! By treating herself with the deepest respect and radical acceptance she could, she would also invite others to naturally do the same! And that's where she discovered the powerful secret of doing shadow work with all your heart, soul, and mind in it.

This was such a wonderful moment of truth she never forgot. She sat in utter shock the day she discovered that her unhealed childhood trauma and emotional wounds kept bleeding into all aspects of her precious life. Rachel would take long walks just thinking deeply about the connection between herself and the dynamics she was experiencing in her turbulent marriage, and she also thought about how her children struggling with so many insecurities and then being dismissive and avoidant were all signs of the unhealed inner child within her desperately pleading for acceptance and love. That feeling of disconnection she had was also a constant reminder of the need for healing and to be taken seriously.

Even though she tried using shortcuts to fix things or tried external strategies like changing geographical locations, blaming others for her problems, changing jobs, and pampering herself, all of it proved futile. Rachel eventually reached a point of no return after trying so hard and realizing that she had to face the real problem head-on. At that breaking point, she knew that it was time to accept the objective truth. That truth was that in all her struggles, there was always one common denominator: her. This astounding perception gave her the strength and courage to uncover more truths and understand what about her had made her create the kind of life she had been living.

Through the loving help of a close friend who had shared with her about shadow work and the incredible results she got, Rachel gained the courage to start her inner healing journey too, but this time with full strength. Her friend helped her realize how true and lasting healing was rooted in facing and loving parts of herself she was rejected all this time. Rachel took her first step in gaining massive self-awareness and unpacking every layer of her past and character. The journey was filled with moments of intense joy and even some days where it was so hard to face what she was seeing about herself. Because of the tremendous amount of work she committed to it, Rachel started to transform like a beautiful caterpillar changing into the most exquisite butterfly. With every step she took, big or small, she could see her life reflect back to her all those positive changes too. It became so exciting.

Imagine waking up every morning knowing you have the key to manifest a specific reality you want. Wouldn't you too be intrigued and happy to create a beautiful life all over again? The joy Rachel felt in her heart was unmatched. As she reflected on the 12 months she spent taking time exploring and working on every part of herself, she was blown away to see the remarkable difference she had made not only in her life but in the lives of her loved ones too. Because Rachel became more by growing into her true self, she now had the capacity for more. She started to give and receive more. She began to attract her wildest dreams too. Connecting to her true self and believing in herself again helped her finally achieve the quality of life she had hoped to live before.

Like Rachel, many of us can find ourselves sinking in the depths of despair, feeling like victims of our own loves. However, this book is here to remind you that it doesn't have to be that way anymore. You hold the keys to unlocking your dreams and making them come true! You already do! All that's needed now is for you to start believing in those keys and learn how to use them. That's where this book comes in. It takes you through the process of navigating all that you may have been running away from. You will learn how to do shadow work through the guidance of effective prompts to use in facilitating your self-reflection, healing, and growth. You will start building the life you've always known you deserved. Just think about what it would be like to finally be your true self! Imagine how fulfilling your days will start to be. Think about all that heavy weight that will get taken off your shoulders now. This journey will leave you feeling lighter and wiser. You will be ready to run and finish your race in style and undisputed triumphant this time! Get ready to meet the real you and deepen your self-love like never before!

Rachel's transformation wasn't an overnight change. Through step-by-step consistent daily efforts, she started to see significant improvements. Everything had a ripple effect! When she stopped judging herself or hiding parts of her, she also started seeing others stop judging her, and they also became more comfortable with showing parts of themselves they would otherwise hide before. Her marriage, which was once difficult due to her unhealed wounds, started to take off on a positive new trajectory. She could sense that their connection was deepening and both of them were now more mindful of how they were showing up for each other. Furthermore, it was so moving to see the change in her children too. As Rachel started growing, her children's emotional well-being also started to improve. They began to exude more self-confidence and show up as their authentic selves. When it came to friendships, her energy became so attractive, as she was now vibrating on a higher positive frequency; people just felt irresistibly drawn to her!

Diving deep into inner child healing and doing shadow work from the core helped Rachel learn that the key to being her true self and loving herself deeply didn't lie in becoming someone else. All she had to do was learn to accept and love who she was. Just like you would pay more attention to a plant that's not doing well and give it extra care instead of hiding and starving it, Rachel knew that her hidden parts were the sides of her that needed her love and support more than anything else. By learning to take care of them and nurture them with love and skill, she would be able to bring out the best that's hidden within those parts. Integrating every piece of who she was became the answer to deepening her self-love. No matter how she had lived before, she knew that what mattered now was to embrace the present and make the most of it. She wouldn't be able to create a new life if she held on to the past. Her tenacity and willingness to invest in this journey of wholeness and mastering true self-love helped her to have so much more to give to her loved ones. She was no longer bleeding into those who didn't traumatize it, as was the norm. Instead, doing shadow work helped Rachel have so much more abundant love to give to herself and others. That's when it dawned on her why the key to loving others is learning to love oneself properly, for we can only give to others what we have.

Like Rachel, you too are about to jump right into that exciting journey of exploring every corner of shadow work. This means you are now on a path of self-discovery and building a true connection with the entirety of who you are. You will master the art of loving yourself deeply. That means you will now become a wellspring of life, love, and light to those around you too. Thank you for choosing to give yourself and others this beautiful gift of learning to unleash the best of you. Are you ready to change things and rewrite your story? I'm sure you are, so let's get right into this and build the lives of our dreams together!

Chapter 1:

The Crucial Starting Point for Transformation: Inner Child Healing

Isn't it awe-inspiring how life is always teaching us something important about ourselves? Often, when things go wrong, it's easy to look outward and blame others. However, doing so makes us give away our power. It makes us powerless to change the situation because there's no guarantee that external factors will change since they are often outside our control. What puts us in a position of power and growth is when we look inward. Taking time to reflect on how we could have contributed to the outcomes we see helps us find answers. By doing this, we can change the trajectory of how things are unfolding and create the outcomes we wish to see. This is what makes the journey of inner child healing so impactful. It's a path of looking inward and learning what it is about ourselves that might be causing us to experience the things we go through. When transformation starts from within, it's the kind of change that lasts forever and brings about phenomenal results.

Shadow work is a journey of achieving wholeness. One of the first steps we can take to attain that wholeness is to heal our inner child. Through this chapter, we will explore guided steps and strategies you can use to navigate this journey seamlessly even if it's your first time hearing about inner child healing. The content is so rich, but it is simple and straight to the point. You will be given effective exercises and steps you can take to reconnect with your inner child; that part of you that reminds you of who you truly are at the core. By walking this road, you also have to get a chance to heal from the past hurts you might still be bleeding from. More than making peace with the past, you will be able to soothe your inner child and learn how to relate to that child better and integrate her into your present daily adult life. You will be able to start bridging the gap that was created when parts of you became split and fragmented in your pursuit of safety, love, and survival. This means you will be able to start reconnecting with the authentic you, no longer having to suppress who you are but instead loving and shining the light of the beauty of your unique spirit. So, yes; it is time to get ready. Once you are mentally prepared to begin this lifechanging journey, we can begin.

Meeting Your Inner Child and Getting to Know Them Better

What does the phrase "inner child" really mean? It's a real part of your psyche that contains all the records of your past experiences, emotional memories, and information about the pure essence of who you are. When we were young, that's when we were most in touch with that pure version of ourselves. However, as time goes on and we experience all sorts of things, the true essence of who we are starts to get diluted by the things we go through. We can start to wear masks or lose touch with our uniqueness. But deep within our psyche, who we are still remains alive. The only problem is that who we are will be trapped inside, rarely allowed to live. It's like someone else takes over our bodies and lives pretending to be the real us when the real us is locked inside, terrified, crying, hurt, and screaming for liberation.

As a result, we grow up feeling very confused and disconnected from ourselves because we live as someone we are not for too long. It may even get to a point where we even believe that's the real us. That's when things get tricky. That's why inner child work is so important. Through it, we can thoroughly unpack what's really going on, find the truth, and take measures to reconnect fully with our true selves represented by our inner child.

To help you understand how our inner child tends to cry out for help, think about times when you reacted to certain situations very strongly to a point where it seemed like your reaction was disproportionate to what happened. Consider times when you would hear unkind remarks from others or just normal criticism, and think about how those moments threw you off and made you feel hurt or angry. Maybe relationships tend to trigger you more than they should. Things that happen or don't happen tend to upset you more than the situation warrants. Maybe you just feel offended easily by things even if the person you were interacting with didn't mean to hurt you. You might then immediately rush to lash out at them or block them, seeing them as a threat even though that may not be the case at all. All such things stem from having a traumatic and unhealed past that indicates that your inner soul is hurting and needs some love and nurturing.

Thus, inner child work is the process of learning to recognize the wounded parts of your soul and making sure that you no longer live a life of neglecting your soul and what it needs. When we don't take time to heal our wounded souls, that's when our adult lives become chaotic and filled with repetitive patterns of the same undesirable experiences. This happens because what we experienced, our hurts and disappointments we faced back then, still influence who we become, how we live, what we do, and how we see ourselves and others. When we overlook those wounds, they still show their face one way or the other. They start to manifest in our adult lives as unhealthy relational habits we have, triggers we have, and insecurities we end up also projecting onto others.

Can you relate to all this? Would you say you've noticed that maybe you keep experiencing the same relationship problems you used to when you were young? Do you ever feel unsafe, unloved, and overlooked like you used to when you were a child? If the answer is "yes," that means you might be reliving the same wounds all over again in your present life; namely, being retraumatized by yourself and other people knowingly or unknowingly. If all this is happening, then don't worry at all. You are at the right place at the right time. Together, we can overcome all pain and open the path to a new future. We will now heed the call of our inner child and try our best to give them the love and care they've always needed and deserved.

Why Is Inner Child Work So Important?

Inner child work is the pathway to learning how to deeply love ourselves. It's hard to love and care for what you don't understand. That's why Inner child work is so fundamental in our self-love journey because through it, we start to understand ourselves, and with understanding comes self-compassion. Instead of judging ourselves so cruelly for our flaws, we can start to realize why we act the way we do. We get enlightenment and learn that so much of who we are now and what we chose to do was all rooted in the quest for survival and trying to cope with the reality of life which is not always rosy.

Childhood events we went through can leave significant imprints on our psyche, especially when those events made us either feel loved or unloved, seen or unseen, misjudged or understood. The cute and joyful experiences we have left a mark on our souls. The people we admired and looked up to become role models who inspired us to dream and work hard to be someone we pictured when we were children. All our past experiences can still affect and influence the way we live our lives and see the world.

Signs of an Unhealed Inner Child

How can we recognize the parts of us that aren't healed yet? In this segment, we will explore different ways we can discover and understand the hurt we still carry within us. Below are some ideas that can help you check the condition of your inner child.

- How often do you feel inadequate or struggle with low self-worth, even if you're doing well?
- Are you temperamental? Do you find it hard to control your emotions? Are you easily angered?
- Do you allow people to just walk over you or use you?

- Do social gatherings make you feel uneasy and anxious to the point where you just prefer isolation?
- Do you often dismiss your emotions or downplay how others feel?
- Do you avoid conflict or run away from uncomfortable emotions?
- Do you crave intimacy but also ferociously push people away?
- Do you downplay yourself and constantly self-sabotage?
- Do you play small and shrink instead of taking space and going for what you want?

These few examples are key tale-tell signs that childhood trauma is still taking the reins and your inner child is hurting. All those behaviors and feelings come from having either a traumatic childhood or not having your needs met. This result is us telling ourselves false stories like, "I'm not good enough," or "I don't deserve to be loved."

To help you connect more with your inner world, take some time to reflect on the many emotions you tend to hide. Try to list 10 in as much detail as you can. Then, list 10 needs you have that you felt were scarcely met, if ever. Emotional suppression and withdrawal from others are all a result of feeling like you can't trust those around you. While this might have been true when you were young. This doesn't have to continue to be your reality. Why? Because now you are grown and your adult self can assure your inner child that it's okay. *I've got your back. I'm here.* That means you can now learn to freely express your needs and be present with your emotions because there's at least one person you can trust... Yourself! Through healing, you can learn to become the parent your inner child never had before.

The Solution: Shadow Work

Shadow work...The term, at first glance, might sound heavy and intimidating because we immediately think of a dark shadow. But trust me, it's really quite just the opposite! Shadow work is a liberating path to healing that drives away darkness from our souls and paves the way for light to illuminate us. It's the journey of learning to recognize, acknowledge, love, and care for the idea of who we are that we often hide from others out of shame and fear. Those rejected parts also represent the wounded parts of our inner child. Why did we hide them? Chances are that it's because something made us believe that they are unlovable or would get us in trouble if we allowed them to come to the surface.

Shadow work helps us dismantle those lies and limiting beliefs. It sheds light on us and helps us create new perspectives that allow us to see our hidden parts for what they truly are; beautiful aspects of who we are that are lovable and worthy!

Through shadow work, we can check the subconscious beliefs that keep our inner child small and hurting. When we learn to embrace and integrate those hidden parts in our holistic lives, they in turn start to heal and grow too. This means that to get started, we have to deeply understand which parts of ourselves we've been ashamed of and have been and suppressing or ignoring. All those sides of who we are desperately need validation, especially from ourselves. To help facilitate that process, let's try out some exercises for emotional release.

Emotional Release Exercise

Our Inner child is carrying the weight of so many emotions that often weigh us down as adults. Releasing those emotions can help us let go of feelings and memories that aren't serving us anymore. Let's get started with some powerful exercises you can do at your earliest convenience.

Visualization

This exercise requires you to travel back to your past and be present with your inner child in the different situations they went through which hurt them deeply. Your inner child probably didn't feel seen, heard, and validated when they felt traumatized or hurt in those situations. So, the role you will play is that of being the supportive parent your inner child needed at that time. This will require you to concentrate very well so that you can vividly recall what happened and be fully present with your inner child. Are you ready?

1. Find a place where you can relax and close your eyes as you imagine who you were back then (your inner child). What happened in your past that made you feel hurt, lost, scared, doubtful, worried, unsafe, or abandoned?

2. Try to describe what was happening as much as you can. You can even record yourself. What matters most is that you now have to be the mouthpiece of your inner child and say in direct speech how you feel. For example, "Mom was so angry when I came home from school. Without explaining why, she just shut the door on my face, made me sit outside starving, and didn't even explain what I had done wrong. This happened on three occasions. Each time, it happened it reinforced in me the belief that mom is unpredictable and I need to keep my distance and always be on guard in case she suddenly blows up again."

3. Reflect on how it affected you. For example, "Now, getting close to people is so hard for me. I just think they will also find it easy to treat me poorly like Mom did. I try not to depend on others because I don't know if things will suddenly change and they will also abandon or treat me poorly for no reason."

4. Once you share how you felt, get in touch with your adult self and reassure your inner child that you are here for them. Tell your inner child *Tell me more*, and make your inner child feel loved, heard, supported, and cared for. Holding space for your inner child's emotions is key to helping those emotions to be processed and released.

5. After your inner child has fully expressed themselves, give them the emotional validation and physical affection they need by hugging yourself and imagining your inner child embracing you and feeling safe in your arms. Promise your inner child that you will try your best to protect and watch over them and encourage them to talk to you whenever they need anything.

You can do this exercise as many times as you need to, especially when you sense that your inner child might be triggered and feeling unsafe.

Emotional Release

Following the previous visualization exercise, you can then journal about the experiences your inner child shared with you. Check how those experiences still affect you in your present life. Details matter. Write as meticulously as you can about everything that happened, how you interpreted things, what you decided to do, how it shaped who you were, and how you showed up thereafter.

You will notice that you might start to get emotional again. That's okay. Allow your emotions to freely flow. After that, you can use affirmations to release any heavy emotions you might have been experiencing. For example, you could say:

- I'm choosing to finally let go of my anger and rage today.
- I choose to share my love with others instead of holding on to resentment and bitterness.
- I'm forgiving everyone who hurt me before and choosing to release them.
- I don't have to be ashamed of myself anymore because I am not defined by my mistakes or flaws.
- It's okay for me to feel this way.
- I choose to fill my heart with kindness, joy, and love.

Notice that doing this frees your heart. Emotions are energy; they don't want to be suppressed. They just grow bigger and more intense when we do so. That's why making time to process them is actually one of the best ways to release them. That way, they can share the messages they need to tell you, and once they are validated, they pass away.

Acknowledging the Gifts, Talents, and Strengths of Your Inner Child

Okay, so now that we've dealt with the painful and hurting side of your inner child, what's next? Exploring your bright side that's all stocked up with gifts and talents.

Inner child work is also about discovering your unique strengths and learning to bring them to the surface. What used to make you happy when you were a child? Where do you think all your present creativity and fun side comes from? Definitely your inner child! Just as children are so spontaneous and always ready to explore and go on adventures, so are you! That side of you is still very much alive and kicking. As you get to connect with your inner child more, you become more in tune with that spontaneous, bold, carefree, fun, and creative side of yourself.

Your inner child actually also remembers so many things you are good at that you may have forgotten about. That's why it's so important to take some time to bond with your inner child. Make sure that you set aside quality time outside your busy adult schedule just to connect with your inside voice and hear what your inner child wants to tell you. Sometimes, they might say, *Hey, why are you so serious? Let's go play and dance!* Guess what? That would be a great opportunity to build trust with yourself and actually do what you love. Maybe you might have shut down that fun side of you. But your inner child can give you the courage and motivation to bring life to that side again. Even if others think of it as silly, it really doesn't matter. What matters most is that you would have honored your true needs and made your inner child happy which is equal to making your authentic self happy too.

You can ask yourself some reflective questions like:

- Which places did I enjoy spending most of my time in?
- What makes me excited and happy?
- What kind of hobbies do I enjoy?
- When did I disconnect from the part of me that loves adventure and play? Why?

Reconnecting with your inner child will require you to no longer shun all those interests. It means starting to do what makes your heart skip with joy even if others think of it as being worthless or silly. As you reconnect with all the parts of your inner child like creativity and play, you will start to feel a sense of wholeness and growth come upon you. That's because you will be getting in touch and integrating once more with all those disconnected parts of who you truly are. It's exciting!

You build trust with your inner child (your true self) by learning to consistently:

- Validate your true emotions.
- Tap into your creative side and embrace adventure.
- Always hold space for your inner child's voice and needs.
- Play and stand up for them when they need your protection.

Activity: Write a Heartfelt Letter to Your Inner Child

One of the most powerful and sweetest ways to have closure and make peace with your inner child is to write them a heartfelt letter. Sincerely acknowledge how they felt and ensure that you help your inner child know that they will never be alone again. They will never have to feel unsafe because you are here to stay. The letter serves as a channel for conveying your deep love for yourself, offering your soul and parts of you that were hurting the assurance that everything is going to be okay. Below are steps you can take to help you through the activity:

- Address your inner child using a sweet, endearing name.
- Acknowledge how they feel.
- Give reassurance.
- Compliment and thank your inner child for never giving up.
- Share your future plans with your inner child.
- Tell them you look forward to walking this journey together and always hearing their voice.

There might be times when you will have an urge to stop and just "go back to normal," but all that sort of resistance is common. Do your best to keep going and even take a break if need to, but be sure to finish writing the letter because just doing that act makes your inner child feel like they are important and their needs matter.

A healthy relationship with your inner child takes time to build. Just like any other relationship, it's not meant to be just a once-off connection. It's a commitment to a new relationship with renewed trust. Just as we all have to go through different stages of knowing those we love, we do the same with ourselves. Your relationship with your inner child will deepen in time, and its quality will all depend on the investment you make daily in making that relationship soar. Just imagine how beautiful life will be, and visualize the peace resulting from no longer being at war with your inner child. It's life-changing!

Chapter 2:

The Road to Deepening Your Self-Love

Do you ever feel like most of your life has been a constant chase for love? Perhaps you grew up feeling a huge void inside you. This might have led you to believe that if only you could find the right person (or people), someone who would just fall madly in love with you or simply accept and validate you just as you are, then you would feel fulfilled and happily ever after. This desire then probably resulted in you chasing for love outside yourself in the hope of one day finding that person or at least making someone love you the way you've always wanted to be loved. If you resonate with this, how would you say that chase has been going? Chances are that it rarely worked well. But why is that so? It's because we have to realize that the love we deeply long for can only come to us once we learn to give it to ourselves first! Feels like a truth bomb, right?

While this might not be how we expected love to work, that's actually how things really work. Let's think about it logically: If you can't give yourself the love you yearn for and you already know how difficult it can be, would it make sense to then expect someone else to easily love you that way? That's why the road to deepening our self-love is truly the answer to attracting the rest of the love we wish to have from others. First, we must learn to love ourselves, and it's through others seeing us recognize the beauty in ourselves that they too will start to see us through our eyes and love us the same. That's why shadow work is one of the best things anyone can do for themselves! Because if we continue to reject ourselves, then the cycle of others rejecting us becomes unending. But if we look within and unlock our capacity to love ourselves, that's what brings about the beautiful love we all desperately long for.

The question now becomes how then do we master the art of self-love seeing that many of us struggle to love ourselves fully? Let's jump into the next section to see how we can build a profound bond with ourselves and love ourselves deeply.

The Core Components of Self-Love

Self-love isn't something we momentarily feel in a fleeting moment once in a while. No. It's actually the way you choose to see and treat yourself every day. It's a lifestyle of choosing specific behaviors that align with valuing yourself. Let's see what some of the key aspects of self-love are that we can embody to build a solid foundation of unwavering trust and love for ourselves.

- **Self-Acceptance:** At the core of self-love is accepting everything that makes you who you are, even your shadow traits.
- **Self-Care:** Whatever we love, we care for. That means constantly nourishing and growing your mind, body, and soul.
- **Self-Belief:** This aspect is rooted in the understanding that before anyone else believes in you, you must first do so. You must believe that you're special and inherently worthy.
- **Self-Compassion:** This aspect is about how you treat yourself. Are you kind and loving to yourself or do you break yourself down?
- **Self-Appreciation:** This entails being able to value and be grateful for everything about you. This means not taking anything lightly and always celebrating who you are.
- **Self-Trust:** This means always having faith in yourself and believing in your ability to make the right choices.

- **Self-Respect:** Whatever we love, we respect. This means not allowing ourselves to play small or allowing others to treat us poorly. Self-respect is about always striving to protect and bring out the best in ourselves.

How Your Self-Love Impacts All Your Relationships: The Mirror Effect

You might have already noticed that the way you treat yourself will always determine how others also perceive and treat you. That means that when we are rooted in self-love and deeply care for ourselves, we're more likely to attract relationships reflecting the depth of love we have for ourselves.

That means if we neglect and don't love ourselves, the chances of finding ourselves in toxic relationships where we will feel neglected are also high. That's when we might keep on being a magnet to relationships that leave us feeling depleted and utterly disappointed. All such damages are there to teach us a valuable truth about life. It all just means that the love we are seeking in others is the exact love we are choosing to withhold from ourselves. So, those relationship dynamics keep repeating all over again even if we find a new partner or new friends. It still happens all over again. Why? Because the underlying problem hasn't been addressed yet; the fact that we first need to learn to love ourselves for others to know how to love us.

Take Mary, for instance. She kept attracting romantic partners who gave her the bare minimum and invalidated her. Even though she would keep giving more and more of herself in the hope that they would love her back more, it only just got worse. She would find herself feeling even more disrespected and love-deprived. It was only after she started doing shadow work that it dawned on her that the reason why she kept attracting toxic people was because of her lack of self-love. Once she dived into learning to nurture her inner child, prioritizing herself and setting very clear boundaries, she experienced a paradigm shift. She was no longer attracting the same experiences to the degree that she used to. The more she kept working on herself, the more the quality of her relationships kept improving. This showed her how, all along, she actually had the key to change things. All she had to do was stop waiting for others to change or forcing them to. She just had to look within and change the way she saw and treated herself. Everything else naturally fell into place after that.

Harnessing Shadow Work to Deepen Your Self-Love

The reason why we sometimes struggle to love ourselves is because of the hidden parts of us we perceive as being unlovable and shameful. When we continue to live according to that narrative, that *There's something wrong with me* mindset, it makes us self-reject and steals our confidence in ourselves. That's where we also start to feel like imposters once anything good lands in our lives. Instead of believing that we deserve it and enjoying that good thing, we end up questioning why it's there and driving it away.

That's why shadow work helps a lot. Because through it, you can make time to analyze and understand all the parts of who you are that you reject. You can bring them to light and start to care for them. Just that act of you accepting those parts and no longer demonizing them causes an energetic shift. It makes you feel so much love for yourself and before you know it, you will also notice others also start to appreciate those parts of you and love you for who you are entirely not just the parts of you that seem to be the best.

Deepening Your Self-Love: Journaling Prompts

We can actively kickstart our shadow work by using journaling prompts to help us self-reflect and get in touch with the deep parts of ourselves that need our love and understanding the most:

- When did I first feel like I wasn't worthy or loved? What happened?
- What did I always long for as a child? Were my needs met? Which needs weren't met and how can I now take charge and meet those needs for myself?
- Are there any destructive beliefs I have that I adopted from my childhood?
- How do I sabotage my relationships when I feel like I'm unlovable and not deserving of happiness?
- Which parts of myself do I feel guilty or ashamed of? Why? How can I start being more accepting of parts of myself that I am not happy with?
- What do I deeply long for? How do I want to be loved? What can I do to give myself that love?
- Do I deprive myself of happiness and fun? Why? How can I start to allow more joy into my life?
- Which feelings do I usually suppress? Why? How can I start expressing them in a more emotionally intelligent way?
- Do I still punish myself for my past mistakes? Why? How can I stop that?
- What do I reject about myself? How can I change that and be more loving to myself?
- When I'm alone, who am I really? Is that the real me? Why do I hide that person from others?
- What would I no longer tolerate if I loved myself deeply and unconditionally?

- How can I be more accepting of my flaws and see them as part of what makes me who I uniquely am?

- Is my shadow side asking me to validate or heal something? What is it?

- How can I start honoring my needs more?

- How can I make sure that my inner child's voice is never ignored again?

- Which dreams do I have that I buried which I now have to go for?

Part of deeply loving ourselves entails learning to reparent our inner child. This means we can now consciously wake up each day knowing that we have full responsibility of looking after ourselves and making sure that we are fully there for our inner child. This responsibility shouldn't be put on someone else's shoulders. It's something only we can do. Our inner child can trust us. We don't have control over how consistent other people are going to be with us, but we have full control over how consistent we can be with our inner child. Just as a responsible parent would have a plan for how they will look after their child, we also have to become very intentional about having a solid plan for looking after our inner child too. This is what's at the core of deepening our self-love. Now, let's move on to another crucial exercise we can use as often as we need to deepen our self-love: Mirror work.

Mirror Work: Learning to See and Acknowledge Your True Reflection

You probably know that one of the hardest things to do when struggling with self-love is to deeply look at yourself. That's because it can remind us of how unhappy we are with what we see, so we just try our best to either avoid looking at the mirror or hide somehow. Mirrorwork helps us enhance our self-love because, through this exercise, you will learn to deeply look within and change the wrong narratives you have about yourself through empowering affirmations. It helps us finally stop criticizing and judging ourselves. All that mean talk is replaced with loving and positive affirmations that lead to self-acceptance and self-appreciation.

To help you get started, you can follow this simple guide:

1. Find some quiet time and stand right in front of your mirror.

2. If you are a lady, make sure you aren't wearing makeup. If you're a man, also make sure you aren't wearing a hat or concealing anything.

3. Directly gaze at your eyes and hold the gaze for a while.

4. Notice any negative thoughts or emotions that come up. What are they saying?

5. Counter those unpleasant thoughts by saying one powerful affirmation at a time while still looking at yourself.

6. If any emotions come up, let them be. Hold space for yourself. Continue to plant life-giving words in your heart and mind through affirmations.

The most powerful affirmations are the ones you wish you could hear someone you love say to you. So, write them down beforehand if you can and then repeat them over and over again until it sinks in. To help you with that, here are some examples of affirmations we wish we could hear from others than you can start saying to yourself:

- I am so beautiful, inside and out.

- I am safe.

- I am proud of who I am and even more proud of who I am growing up to be.

- My emotions matter. I listen to them and take responsible action.

- I am my unfailing source of love and joy.

- Every part of me deserved to be seen and loved.

- I love the way I live my life.

- I am an amazing gift to this world.

Gratitude Journaling

Next, a powerful tool to deepen our self-love is gratitude journaling. This means instead of allowing negative thoughts to dominate us all day long, we can shift our focus to what we are grateful for. This helps you validate and acknowledge yourself which makes you less desperate to get that acknowledgment from others. When you do get it, it will just be a bonus, not something you need to feel worthy.

Each day, you can record:

- Two things you are grateful for that day.

- Two things you did to nourish and love yourself that day.

- Two new things you are proud of learning that day.

- Two things you did to make your inner child happy that you are proud of.

Lastly, making sure that we place the right limits is also key to protecting ourselves. Boundaries aren't only about saying "no" to others. They also entail learning to say "yes" to everything that helps us grow and become our best selves. Make time to identify areas where you might have been playing small and start to push yourself to grow. Also, find respectful ways to teach others how to treat you well.

Self-care is a non-negotiable when it comes to deepening your self-love. Make time each day to ensure that your body, spirit, and soul are well looked after. Take inventory every night of what you did to care for yourself before you sleep. As you make this your lifestyle, you will notice just how exciting and enriching it is to be attuned to your needs and also massively invest in yourself. You become very attractive and more abundance starts to naturally gravitate towards you, including love!

Chapter 3:

Exploring Your Shadow Self

Now, it's time for us to dig deeper into our shadow selves and see what's really going on. How often do you catch yourself being strongly triggered by something and only later wonder *Hey, that was quite a strong emotional response I had to that situation. Why did that affect and offend me so much?* It can feel very unsettling knowing that we've reacted in those ways, and we might even want to just quickly forget about it. But what if that's where your breakthrough lies? What if that's exactly what you have to zoom into and analyze to find the answers you're looking for? Those moments of intense display of our emotions often mirror our shadow sides that we hide and suppress. Instead of seeing those times as moments of weakness, we can start seeing them as loving and earnest reminders from our shadow selves to pay more attention to what's going on inside us and help ourselves heal.

When we stop running away from our shadows and begin to look deeply into ourselves, we will be able to learn so much about who we are and what we are capable of. What's exciting about shadow work is that it reveals to us the secret to unleashing our greatness. It all lies in no longer avoiding ourselves and instead learning to relate to our shadow self in a way that's empowering and life-changing.

Origins of Shadow Work and Its Purpose

Carl Jung, a psychologist who popularized the theory of shadow work, described the "shadow" as parts of who we are that we believe to be unlovable or not acceptable, and as a result, parts we end up hiding. However, understanding the shadow correctly can help us no longer see it as our enemy or the source of all our problems. We will begin to notice how the shadow is actually that part of ourselves that holds our unlimited potential and represents our uniqueness. It's the source of our creativity and even our strengths. Embracing those neglected parts helps us feel whole and more connected to ourselves. When people relate to us, we will start to feel more connected if we also allow them to know our shadow self.

Jung shared that the shadow represents parts of our personality that we are often unconscious of. Why do we refuse to acknowledge those parts? It's often because we fear that doing so will get us in trouble or make others reject us. The belief that those parts will make us unloved and feel unworthy is what makes us bent on constantly suppressing those parts even when we know that it's hurting us. Nevertheless, the exciting news is that once we break free from those limited beliefs, we are able to start unearthing our shadow selves and learning to integrate them effectively into our daily lives.

Shadow work is a sweet and loving journey of learning to discover and love parts of who you are that already exist. That means no judgment; all you do is just engage with your shadow self from a place of love and compassion. Through that journey, we learn to appreciate everything about ourselves and understand that for us to be our best, we need that diversity within us. Everything can't all be the same. Your flaws aren't meant to harm you; when treated with wisdom, they can become your greatest strength.

Take for example someone who knows they are lazy. They might hide that aspect from others, but when they're alone, they fall back into that trait. What that can do for them is that since they don't like working hard, that lazy side of them can start to stir up so much creativity within them. They can start to think of various ways to automate their workflow so that they don't have to do heavy manual labor every day. Instead, they can become innovative and come up with unconventional ways to get things done. Ways that require very minimal effort. So, in retrospect, their shadow self, while seen as a flaw by others, actually turns out to be their biggest strength. It inspires them to be one of the greatest innovators! Pretty cool stuff, right?

Now, just imagine what you could achieve through your shadow self if only you stop running away from it. Think about how creative you will start to become. Imagine how liberating it will feel to no longer feel bad for being who you are. Instead, you just see it as an opportunity to grow and make positive contributions to yourself and others.

Benefits of Doing Shadow Work

- **Authenticity:** Authenticity is one of our biggest human needs. Shadow work helps us to live more authentic lives. Instead of acting like someone you're not, you start to show up as your true self. This can be very liberating and even socially appealing. People are drawn to someone who isn't ashamed of being who they truly are. There is so much weight that gets lifted off your shoulders when you accept yourself.

- **Successful Relationships:** Accepting your shadow also helps you to no longer punish or treat others poorly because of your shadow self. Often, if we don't own our shadow, we end up just blaming others for our flaws and projecting our insecurities on them. This means that we become more responsible and self-aware people. This leads to healthier and more harmonious relationships.

- **Empathy:** When we acknowledge our shadow, we start to also understand other people's shadows and judge them less. Empathy takes root. We start to understand that all of us are wounded and are trying to heal. This gives birth to more compassionate behavior towards others.

- **Healing:** All those emotions we might have spent years burying can finally be addressed, leading to emotional healing. We start to have a healthier emotional landscape. We can also become more emotionally available to ourselves and others.

- **Self-Awareness:** We start to live mindful lives, being more aware of what might hurt others or ourselves, thus choosing more responsible behavior. Things that used to hold us back become clearer and we become more empowered to break free from negative behavioral cycles.

Now, let's think about what happens when we don't do shadow work and just choose to continue on the way we have been living. The outcome is scary to even think of. Here are examples of behaviors we may find ourselves repeating:

- We attract and maintain toxic relationships.
- We live the rest of our lives disconnected from ourselves and unable to form deep and intimate connections with others.
- We remain bloodied from our wounds.
- We continue to blame and project our insecurities and flaws on others.
- We judge others harshly and push people away.
- We struggle with mental health issues like anxiety and stress from unresolved emotional pain.

The list goes on. I'm sure that's certainly not a life you would want to continue to live. No wonder it becomes hard to love ourselves or attract love when we haven't done our work. It's really difficult to cultivate healthy relationships when our internal landscape is in that condition. The only way good fruit can sprout from your garden is if the soil is well taken care of. That means, similarly, we too have to focus on healing ourselves in order for us to be fertile ground for positive outcomes to manifest in our lives.

But Where Does the Shadow Self Come From?

I'm sure you've often wondered where your shadow self must have come from. I bet you still remember those childhood days when your soul was so pure and free from all the shadow weight you are carrying now.

Our shadow self starts to develop in our childhood years. As negative experiences unfold in our lives, they all create a new version of us that's broken. For example, being laughed at for crying when you're hurt can make you develop a hardcore rigid personality where you choose to be mechanical and dismiss your emotions. When you see others crying, you can start to judge and criticize them without even realizing where that's coming from.

Our cultures, societal pressures, and family dynamics all contribute too to the creation of our shadow self.

Common Components of the Shadow Self

Since we already touched earlier on what the shadow self comprises, we will just have a brief recap in this segment on what your shadow self is made of for your convenience.

- **Negative Projections:** The things we don't like in others are usually traits we already have that we hide.
- **Unresolved Trauma:** All the wounds within us that haven't been processed and healed.
- **Downplayed Gifts:** Things we are good at that we are afraid of tapping into due to the self-doubt or fears planted in us.
- **Suppressed Emotions:** All kinds of different emotions that we are ashamed of surfacing. For example, anger, anxiety, fear, and desire.
- **Culture Shadows:** Sides we have that we don't show to others because maybe it doesn't fit with the prevailing culture of where you are.

Bringing Your Shadow Self to Light

With our newly found clarity on what shadow work entails and how it's been affecting us, let's now dive right into doing the work and seeing how we can get on the right footing. Bringing your shadow to light will require you to be more accepting and patient with yourself. You will also have to embrace vulnerability and be willing to admit to things that are difficult for you to accept. What's great about this process is that it really works! Yes, it's not always going to be easy, but the reward is well worth the cost we have to pay! Are you ready to jump right in and start setting free your shadow-harnessing wisdom?

30-Day Bringing Your Shadow to Light Journaling Prompts

1. Which character traits do I despise most in others? Do I also have those traits?
2. Which emotions did I feel when I was triggered? What truths were exposed at that moment about me?
3. How do I take criticism? Do I show any hint of insecurity? Which ones are they?
4. Which parts of who I am do I often hide? Where did those parts come from?
5. Which side of my character do I hide because I'm afraid people will judge me?
6. Which feelings and emotions do I usually suppress? Why?
7. Do I struggle with envy? What does that envy show me about my hidden desires?

8. Which behaviors do I think are acceptable because of what was instilled in me by my family or culture?

9. Which side of me do I resist the most? What's the worst and best that could happen if I accept that side?

10. Which strengths and gifts do I have that I downplay because of fear of failure or judgement?

Throughout your 30-day period, you can keep reflecting on these questions. Some will require more time; that's why I only put 10 prompts. Quality is what matters, not rushing through many things. So, focus on having very detailed answers to those questions and enhancing your self-awareness.

An exercise you can do to help you also acknowledge your shadow self is to write down the things you usually project on others. You can find these out by thinking of all the assumptions you have about people. Putting aside these projections can help you learn to connect to people for who they truly are, and not through faulty lenses.

How do you feel so far? I bet you're already starting to feel great about your progress. You deserve to! Congratulations on coming this far, but we still have more work to do. Well done for diving into the work and following through. Let's keep going and make the most of our journey!

Chapter 4:

Effectively Integrating Your Shadow Self Into Your Everyday Life

The main objective of integrating the shadow self into our daily lives is to incorporate a plot twist into the game of life. While the shadow self may seem like it's what hinders you from being your best self, we've already seen that if we connect with that side of us from a place of mindfulness, healing, and love, it can work to our advantage. What you perceive to be your biggest obstacles can turn out to be detours on your path of success that will lead you to levels of victory you might have never imagined before! We do that by tapping into the good we can draw from our shadow traits.

Just think about it; up until now, you've probably lived a life of constantly battling with your shadow side and having a hard time loving yourself deeply because of it. But what if we can decide to make today our turning point? Instead of harboring so much resentment towards your shadow self, you can start to see those seemingly dark parts of you as being your allies instead of your enemies there to hinder your progress. How can we achieve that? By loving every part of ourselves! Everything. I know, it may seem impossible, but in reality, when we allow ourselves to understand those parts instead of judging them, we cannot help but feel so much empathy and compassion for them. It's at that place of understanding, that we can start to build a positive relationship with our shadow selves.

What's beautiful about loving something, be it people or anything else, is that you will want the best for it. You will want to see who or what you love happy. Similarly, the key to deepening our self-love is to allow ourselves to grow our love for our shadow self. Naturally, anything we love, we tend to take care of. So, that means that by choosing to love your shadow self each day, you will start to do things that help those parts of you to develop and grow. This means over time, they no longer remain underdeveloped and seemingly potential threats. They start to be your biggest strength because they have so much to give since they have been shut off for too long.

This is why you would see that writers who are able to tap into their shadow selves and write from their hearts turn out to produce the best books, movie scripts, and songs. It's phenomenal!

Now just imagine what your shadow self is ready to help you build in your life. Maybe you've had a lot of pent-up anger within you because of facing many injustices in your life. Instead of seeing that angry part of you as an undesirable bad side, you can use that to your advantage. You can mindfully tap into that anger, feel it, and use it to come up with creative ways to end injustices wherever you might have seen them prevail. Such is how your shadow self can help you enrich your life when handled wisely. Hiding those parts of us just perpetuates our pain and keeps us average.

In this chapter, we will unpack more ways we can stop being trapped in patterns of self-sabotage and constant emotional distress due to our inability to handle our shadow selves effectively. Your biggest tool for achieving this goal will be the shadow integration process. Let's find out more about it.

What Does Shadow Integration Practically Mean?

Our shadows come to light more often than we might realize. Sometimes, it happens when we have sudden bursts of anger, feelings of envy, jealousy, rage, bitterness, self-doubt, or feelings of inadequacy. What's usually your first response to these emotions when they arise? Chances are that you might instantly try to shove them away. And that's exactly where we now have to learn to do things differently. Instead of hiding that side of us, shadow integration means learning to embrace it and welcome what we see with a mindset of curiosity and determination to use it for good.

Shadow integration means bringing our shadow to our conscious awareness. Doing this helps us have more control of the emotions and triggers we have because of our shadow. So, instead of judging the jealousy you might see arising in yourself and acting like it doesn't exist, you can use a different approach and be curious about it instead. Try to find out which hidden needs and desires you have that you have been burying. Chances are that that's what your jealousy might be teaching you. By acknowledging those desires and unmet needs, you can become more empowered to take a healthy course of action. For example, instead of now trying to pull down someone you are jealous of, you can choose to celebrate their success and see them as a source of inspiration for you to also start achieving the hidden desires they reminded you about. You can even take a further step and ask for advice on ways you can also make it like they did. In that way, acknowledging that shadow side of you would have helped you become more authentic with yourself and achieve something meaningful. Not only will you stand a chance to win your goals, but you will also possibly gain a new friend by communicating with that person and sharing how much you would appreciate their help in aiding you to also achieve the same good outcome.

What other opportunities can you think of that you can use to connect to your shadow self in a healthy way and use it to grow? I'm sure their many times you can think of when you reacted negatively instead of using your shadow self to teach you more about what you needed to know about yourself.

Each day, you can start to journal moments you catch your shadow coming to the surface. Listen carefully to the messages your shadow is telling you. Find the most constructive way to respond to that feedback. Doing this will help you no longer be at war with yourself and others. Instead, it creates inner harmony and becomes a bridge for building very positive and progressive relationships with others. Just think about the depth of emotional freedom you will experience once you start to constructively engage with your shadow self. There's no doubt that by doing this, your love for your shadow self will naturally start to grow stronger each day (which means you will love yourself and others even more)!

More Ways to Constructively Integrate Your Shadow

How can we start integrating our shadow traits? A good place to begin is by understanding that most traits we often consider to be bad, like the ones we discussed in the previous section, are just signals. They aren't bad. What makes those emotions bad is the course of action we then decide to take after experiencing them. Emotions are merely carriers of messages from our hearts and inner child. In this case, those emotions will be carrying messages that our shadow self wants us to know. They are not there to hurt you. Believing that those emotions are bad is what causes us to hide them and disregard what they want to tell us. Doing this is what blocks growth. So, the next step would be to no longer block emotions from your shadow self. Instead, give them your listening ear. Hear what they have to say. Write it down as often as you can. Over time, you will notice that there might be patterns you will start to see. Messages you ignore will keep coming back over and over again. But messages you accept and do something productive about rarely ever come back and pressure us to address the unmet need again.

Think about how kids react when they are ignored. To get your attention, they can quickly become very difficult, throw a tantrum, and even be feisty. Such is how our shadow self can act when we ignore it. It starts to fester and try it's best to surface. Unfortunately, that's when it often comes out in very harmful ways such as projecting those emotions onto others, engaging in self-sabotaging behaviors, and having very unhealthy relationship dynamics.

Integrating the shadow means you get to befriend it and respect what it has to say. That way, it no longer keeps fighting you and wreaking havoc in your life just to get your attention and have its needs met.

Another remarkable advantage of embracing and constructively integrating your shadow is that you get to become a light wherever you go. In your family and friendships, you are able to become the person who brings in healing energy instead of perpetuating destructive behavioral cycles. As you heal and interact with yourself and others from a place of love, you inadvertently also teach others how to heal. This creates a ripple effect. Generations that might have continued on the cycles of unhealthy relationship patterns are then saved from experiencing the severity of passed-on traumas. This is because healthy parents often raise healthy children. When those children grow older, they also teach their children the healthy ways they learned. It becomes a generational culture to love deeply and know how to manage the shadow self effectively.

Integration is truly amazing. It allows you to rewrite your own script and by doing this, you no longer do things in the unhealthy ways your parents and ancestors might have handled things. You no longer have to carry all the weight of the fears, anxiety, and pain they might have projected on you. It's truly the answer to paving a new path that leads to deep healing and true love.

Remember to also always make your triggers your allies and teachers. Continue to allow them to give you great insight into what you can do to become a better person and heal.

Exercises for Constructively Integrating the Shadow

With your newly found awareness of your shadow, the next step is to take action, which will help you to have impeccable results. Let's have a look at different practical action steps you can take to positively engage with your shadow self daily.

- **First Exercise:** Reframe your shadow traits. As discussed, see the good in what your shadow traits are telling you. For instance, if it's envy, then see it as your shadow self reminding you of the unleashed potential you have within you. And fear can be an opportunity for you to explore your hidden courageous and bold side. Do this for the rest of any shadow traits you have.

- **Embrace Vulnerability:** Sometimes, we hide our shadow selves thinking that telling others about it will push them away. While this can happen sometimes, it often actually leads to more enriched connections. People sense how authentic you are, and it also makes them feel safe to be vulnerable with you about their shadow self too. So, whenever you discover something about your shadow, talk about it with others from a place of self-acceptance and empowerment, not criticism. Being critical of your shadow self will likely only invite more criticism from others too. So, the more compassion and curiosity you have about your shadow, the more likely others will also take on that exploration and growth approach. Being vulnerable about your shadow also creates a space where you are finally able to allow yourself to be seen for who you truly are, which is super fulfilling!

- **Change How You See Others:** As we shared earlier on, it's really true that often, what we find irritating and dislike in others is usually traits we also have that we struggle to love and accept about ourselves. That's why we end up judging others because we already judge ourselves very harshly. Being aware of this phenomenon can help us understand that the degree to which we judge and don't accept others is actually how deeply we judge and don't accept ourselves. The key to loving others still remains as loving ourselves first (especially our shadow parts).

This work is truly incredible! Can you imagine that all the judgment you had for yourself and others mostly came from you not accepting your shadow self? Now, think about how your energy and relationship dynamics are going to radically shift the moment you start integrating your shadow traits positively. The compassion and understanding you show yourself daily becomes the compassion and understanding you can also give to others daily. Each day becomes an amazing opportunity to paint your life with bright and warm colors once again. What a beautiful life that would be.

Chapter 5:

Harnessing the Beauty and Power of Creative Expression Hobbies and Activities

Shadow work doesn't have to be serious. You can also consider exploring fun ways to do it. One of those fun gateways to discovering and expressing your shadow self is undoubtedly creative activities. Through them, you can connect with your shadow and express what that shadow looks like. It's a beautiful way of always giving a voice to your buried emotions, hopes, and dreams.

Expressing yourself creatively can happen in diverse ways. Let's have a peek at this list of some forms of creative self-expression activities you might like:

- Interior designing
- Sculpting and pottery
- Baking
- Writing (journaling)
- Music
- Dancing
- Painting

- Crafting
- Film making
- Fashion designing
- Gardening
- Blogging
- Calligraphy

Which activities do you think you would enjoy the most? Maybe you can also take a moment to brainstorm some activities that resonate best with your spirit. Creativity is a helpful avenue to help us release any buried feelings and express ourselves better. This makes it therapeutic. It can also create an atmosphere supportive of cultivating self-awareness and growth. Maybe you struggle to express yourself verbally. You are ready to be seen by others and also free yourself in your eyes, but words aren't your strength yet. You can use creative expression to help you still achieve your communication and healing goals. It's a great aid, especially when we want to say something we feel we may be failing to articulate properly.

Think of your creativity as being a helpful connecting rope between your conscious mind and the deepest parts of your shadow self that are crying out to be heard, seen, and set free.

Your creative hobbies and activities can be valuable times you get to dive in and explore your inner world. You get to understand all those suppressed desires, fears, worries, insecurities, dreams, and emotions that shape who you are today. As you allow yourself to use your creative avenues as mirrors to help you see and understand yourself better, you will be able to start building a deeper and better relationship with yourself and love all of you.

Activities like drawing, digital art, painting, and even singing can be a powerful mirror to help us express a wide range of emotions. By using varying intensities of colors and shades, you can communicate the depth of what you are expressing to the world. Similarly, with music, there are times you can change your voice tone to convert and match the emotions you wish to communicate. You can also do this with the choice of instruments you decide to use. For instance, an electric guitar can make it very easy to convey emotions like rage or disappointment. While on the other hand instruments like a flute or piano can also be used to convey a mixture of different emotions, both soft and strong.

By regularly engaging in these different activities, we can begin a new and healthier lifestyle of validating our emotions and living an authentic life where we are true to and connected with ourselves. If there are any specific lessons we are struggling to grasp from our shadow, consistently engaging in those activities can help us eventually gain clarity and a deeper understanding of what's really going on within us.

Activities and Exercises for Reviving Your Playful Soul

Do you remember how playful and creative you used to be as a child? Maybe partly. Don't worry; there's someone who still does remember everything vividly if your conscious mind forgot. Guess who that is? Yes, it's your inner child!

All that creative and adventurous energy is stored up within your innermost parts. It's often suppressed as we grow older because of the limiting beliefs we often adopt and other life pressures we find ourselves facing. However, that playful side is still a crucial part of who we are that our spirits long to embrace and tap into. What makes us fully authentic is also reviving that playful side of us. This segment will now guide us on how to do so through creative ideas we can try out.

Below are some adjustments you can consider making to your life:

- **Ensure play time is slotted into your daily schedule:** Often, our adult schedules can be jam-packed with so many things that don't have anything to do with play. This can eventually make us feel drained from our lifestyles and disconnected from ourselves. To do things better, consider incorporating activities you enjoy into your daily routine. It doesn't have to be long. Even just 20 or 30 minutes of dance, drawing, or doing crafts can be a great way to connect with yourself better.

- **Take pictures:** Photography is a beautiful way of capturing special and everyday moments in our lives. It's a creative way you can share your life story in many ways. What can make this therapeutic is taking photos that are not only all polished up and "perfect" but also silly, random, and candid pictures that represent the true reality of our human lives, which are filled with all sorts of daily adventures and challenges. Having a photo album with that kind of authentic and raw photography can serve as a great reminder that there's always something special about the seemingly imperfect moments of our lives. It will also help you celebrate your growth in spontaneity and learn to accept yourself and your life as it is.

- **Finger painting:** Imagine a kid with paint all over their hands, stamping it on paper or walls. Think about how fun that is. Consider also having a paint day where you can just tap into your uninhibited energy and use your creativity to paint something beautiful on a board or somewhere safe.

- **Pillow fights:** When did you last have a slumber party or night out with the boys just playing games? Consider having a cozy evening once in a while to bond with your friends in pajamas. You can do pillow fights or play games that allow you all to connect deeply with your playful spirits.

What helps us to be creative is not being afraid to get messy. Before the perfect idea is born, we must embrace the process's messiness and just learn to enjoy every step. So, while you do any of the creative activities you have in mind, don't worry about perfection. What matters most is just having fun and connecting with your innermost soul. For instance, if you like dance, you don't have to worry about getting every move right. Just focus on ensuring that you are out of your head and just flowing with the rhythm.

What makes us so overly concerned about doing things perfectly? Often, it's a result of experiencing childhood trauma whereby maybe you were punished or shown less affection whenever you weren't perfect according to your caregiver's standards. So, what can help is dismantling that belief and need to be perfect by realizing that you don't have to be perfect for you to be worthy of love. Even when you are making mistakes, you are still lovable! Start to retrain your mind by being more accepting of yourself, especially when things aren't perfect. That's why creative expression activities are a great way to practice that because they give you a chance to embrace the messiness of things and find the fun in them.

The Role Your Imagination Can Play in Shadow Work

Every day, your shadow speaks to you. Before doing our healing work, the relationship between our shadow and our conscious self was likely very toxic. However, through imagination, we can start to shift things. You can use your imagination to start rebuilding a healthy relationship between your conscious self and your shadow. You can do that daily by imagining your conscious mind talking to your shadow. You can even speak out loud (your conscious self) as you respond to the messages you are hearing from your shadow. This new relationship can grow with time, and as your shadow self and conscious self learn to understand, respect, and get along well with each other, your self-love and inner harmony will also deepen.

Another way to harness your imagination is through guided imagery and visualization. Find any soothing or helpful guided meditation sessions you can use to help you interact with your shadow better. Meditation is also a great way to help you understand your emotions and create an environment where you can come up with some creative ideas of what to do for fun.

Consider play as a fundamental part of your self-love journey. Don't see it as something immature. We all have a childlike side inside of us that always yearns for play. Start seeing play as your way to love and cherish that side of yourself.

As we wrap up this chapter, think about all the fun you can start injecting into your life moving forward. Play will help you loosen up and learn to freely just be yourself. So, dive right deep into it and watch how much your inner child will love you more!

Chapter 6:

The Mind-Body Dance: Somatic Awareness

Have you ever experienced all sorts of discomfort or aches in your body that you suspect might be connected to the emotional distress you may be having? If you have, your intuition is right. Our bodies are like living archives that contain the entirety of our day-to-day experiences. That means if you're sad or happy, your body keeps a record of that, and the emotions associated with that experience also get stored in the body.

Did you know that different emotions we have can be felt through various parts of your body? For instance, when you're afraid, you might feel your gut twisting. When you're stressed, you may feel that on your shoulders. So much we go through is felt in many parts of our bodies. But sometimes we dismiss those signals because of uncertainty regarding where they all come from.

Our shadow carries most of our pain and hidden emotions, but where do we get to feel all that pain? In our body. That's why through this chapter, we will explore how we can use somatic awareness to help us understand ourselves more and be more equipped to look after ourselves better.

Somatic awareness is a transformative and effective way to heal. It's done through intently listening to our bodies and the messages being conveyed (Kelsay, 2023). It's like your body is a wellspring of insurmountable wisdom that's waiting for you to pay attention to it. Are you ready to look after yourself and heal from the pain of repressed emotions? I believe you are! Let's start.

Using Somatic Awareness for Shadow Work

The heart of the practice of somatic awareness is consciously listening and tuning into your bodily sensations and what you are feeling. This is done because our bodily sensations usually signal to us the state of our emotional landscape. Did you know that every day, our bodies try to communicate with us? If our bodies like something, we will feel positively about it. Likewise, if our bodies don't like something, we will feel negatively about it. The body sends signals from our conscious mind to tell us what's wrong and urge us to take action. However, when we don't take action and just ignore messages from our shadows being communicated through our bodies, that's when things get messy. Our bodies start to protest and push us to take action by causing us to feel tension, pain, or discomfort in one way or another.

Almost any part of your body that suddenly starts to feel some type of way is trying to communicate with you and let you know that something is not okay. For instance, even just feeling tension in your neck can be a sign of your unprocessed emotions fighting to surface. It's hard to understand what is going on when we aren't mindful. That's why through the practice of somatic awareness, you will be able to decode most of the messages that your body is trying to tell you.

Since one of the biggest aspects of shadow work is understanding our suppressed emotions and needs that we might have been scared to be open about, you can only imagine how somatic awareness will help! Through it, we can understand better how our shadow side releases all that pain and those emotions through our bodies in the form of body aches, tension, tightness, and uneasiness. By regularly paying attention to how your body feels, you can start to address what's going on within you.

Sometimes, we try to force our minds to forget our pain and discomfort. While we can succeed to some degree in achieving that by redirecting our focus to something else, the emotions and memories don't just disappear. They get stored in the body. For instance, feelings of anxiety can be felt through our stomach. When we are going through heartbreak, we often experience it by feeling the pain in our chest.

That means if your stomach and chest are feeling that way, you can know that you need to do something to heal from your anxiety or find comfort to soothe the pain that's coming from your heartbreak. Doing this regularly can also help you to integrate your shadow self more into your everyday life and no longer keep it buried and exiled.

Whenever we hear about trapped emotions, what comes to mind? Usually, it means that a part of how we authentically feel wants to come out, but through adaptive strategies, we end up suppressing those emotions. The result is that we end up showing up as an inauthentic version our ourselves (false self).

Our true selves are who we were born as and what we naturally feel. On the other hand, the false self gets created through a combination of adaptive strategies we develop to cope with pain, rejection, and loss. All of that repressed emotional energy ends up finding another way to come out. Guess how it often gets expressed? Examples include:

- feeling bitter and resentful
- rage
- fatigue
- numbness
- feeling like you aren't real and then avoiding others because of shame
- bad judgment
- compulsive behavior
- depression
- overreacting to things

- indulging in self-sabotaging behaviors
- more stress and anxiety

Where Trapped Emotions Are Stored in the Body

Did you know that different parts of your body store all kinds of different emotions you have (Ishler, 2024)? Knowing exactly where different emotions get trapped can help you understand why you might be experiencing physical challenges in certain body parts. We will have a look at some of the main emotions that get trapped in our bodies.

- **Happiness:** All over your body.
- **Sadness:** Mainly the chest and your head. To a small extent, also in your legs, arms, and feet.
- **Fear:** Mainly in your upper body (except the arms). Sometimes, you will also feel it in your feet.
- **Love:** All over your entire body, but less in the legs.
- **Surprise:** In your chest and your head. Sometimes in the legs to some extent.
- **Depression:** Mainly in your lower body.
- **Anxiety:** Above your pelvis. Less activation in your feet, arms, and legs.
- **Contempt:** In your head as well as your hands. You will feel less activation in your legs and pelvis.
- **Disgust:** Entire upper half of the body.

- **Anger:** Less activation in the feet and legs. You will mostly feel it in the upper half of your body and in your arms too.
- **Shame:** Mainly in your head and torso. You will experience less activation in your legs, arms, and feet.
- **Envy:** Mainly in your chest and head. Less activation in your legs.

Something important to remember is that all the emotions we don't process don't disappear. They get stored in our unconscious minds and bodies. That's why they end up also affecting our posture. To test this, try paying attention to what your posture is like when you're experiencing different emotions. When you're happy and confident, it's likely that your body language will be more open and you take up more space. But when you feel afraid, defeated, or sad, your spine takes a different form; you're likely to take up less space become more slouched and have your head down. Having that said, imagine how your demeanor and body language will change when you start using your shadow work journey to process those repressed emotions healthily! You will start to see the real confident and more self-assured version of you come up and it will show through the way you carry yourself. That's something hopeful you can certainly look forward to!

How to Effectively Listen to Your Body: Body-Scan Meditation

You know how we often hear that it's so important to look after our body, spirit, and soul. Sometimes when it comes to the body, we mainly just think of taking care of it in the form of exercise, sleeping, and eating healthily. But what if there's another very essential way to also look after your body? Something your body desperately needs. What is that way? You probably guessed it right! It's through somatic awareness practices. One of the best ways to do so is through doing a body-scan meditation.

A body-scan meditation is a very simple yet effective way to listen to your body. It involves an internal way of listening to yourself without any judgment. All you have to do is give your body the space and time to communicate with you without any interruptions. It's like saying to your body, "Hey, I care about you so much. I just thought of checking up on you today to find out if you're okay and if you need anything specific from me. I'm all ears." Imagine if we actually set aside even just 10 minutes each day to do this for ourselves. How much more would our bodies love us and feel less stressed or tense?

The body-scan meditation allows us to untangle any problematic knots of emotions we may be carrying. You can release most of the tension you feel through this practice. Through the scan, you can make time for every part of your body, from head to toe. To help you get started on how to do it, let's review a few steps you can take:

1. Sit or lie down in a very serene and comfortable place.

2. Calm your body by taking a few breaths and then close your eyes.

3. Start to fully scan your body using your mind and tuning into how you feel. Bring your attention to each part of your body, from your head to your toes.

4. Take note of what you're sensing. Is there any tension anywhere? Any tightness, warmth, or tingling sensations you feel, note them down.

5. Continue to scan every part one by one and pay more attention to those parts you notice might be tense. Take deep breaths and imagine releasing the tension with each exhale.

6. You can scan in this order if you want: head, shoulders, chest, arms, stomach, thighs, legs, feet, and back.

7. Finish off by taking slow deep breaths, and once you feel your body relaxed, proceed to acknowledge every message you received and wrap up the session with a grateful heart for getting this feedback.

Curiosity is key when scanning your body. Always have an open mind and accept whatever feedback you get.

Emotional blocks usually reside wherever our bodies have the most stress and tension. Whenever you notice that a certain emotion is surfacing, you can name it and reflect on what could have caused it. Body scan meditations can be very helpful in aiding the body to be more relaxed and uncover so much about your shadow, which facilitates deep healing.

How to Unblock Suppressed Energy

When you feel like you're ready to release any negative emotions, guess what you can do? Move! Isn't it amazing how simply moving can be so therapeutic and help unblock suppressed energy? But how does it work? It works by allowing emotions to flow. Remember they're energy, so doing things like jogging, running, swimming, or dancing can be very helpful in relieving suppressed emotions. Even just moving freely without any clear coordination can help. What matters most is to get your body in motion and let the energy flow. What's amazing about the body is that it knows exactly what it feels and needs. What's left is for us to cultivate the habit of learning to listen well to what it says.

Dancing is one of the best ways to help your body release pent-up emotions. Depending on how you feel, you could pick all kinds of different dance styles to release emotions and express how you feel. It could be slow and stretchy moves or fast moves that are more energetic and firm. You could also do this as you listen to your favorite music. Notice how your emotional state shifts. What do you feel when you dance? What did you discover about yourself through the emotions that arose? Remember Rachel from earlier on? Let's find out about how she was able to successfully do her shadow work by harnessing the power of somatic awareness.

Rachel's Successful Shadow Work Journey Through Harnessing Somatic Awareness

Before and after starting her family, Rachel had always stood out amongst her peers as a high-achiever. She was so proud of always being someone reliable and good at managing things. People adored her work ethic and admired her thriving career and personal life. However, what troubled Rachel was that beyond all that exterior was an inexplicable weight she was carrying. She would always feel ongoing tension in her body. Her shoulders were often hunched and tight. Her posture was not the best at all, and she would often have recurring migraines that troubled her.

One night as she was struggling to sleep, she decided to research ways she could find some relief for her aching body. She thought of going for a spa date and then decided to visit a wellness retreat that had educational seminars about somatic awareness. Excited to start her trip, she took the following week off, filled with hope and anticipation for what she was about to learn.

Once she arrived, they were guided in a body-scan meditation session. She closed her eyes, took controlled, deep breaths, and began to navigate her attention to all parts of her body. While fully tuned into the process, she began to notice that her body was so numb. She felt this was very odd. She couldn't feel much happening in the middle section of her body. It was almost as if she was disconnected from most of her body parts.

She became very emotional as she realized that something was wrong and her body had been in so much pain. She started crying; the kind of cry you have when you feel so heartbroken with the state of your spirit and body and you realize that things aren't okay. She was desperate to know what was wrong. Happy with the results from her first session, she decided to take on more sessions days later. Every day, the scan made her feel like she was discovering another piece of the puzzle to who she really was.

During one of her regular sessions, she suddenly experienced a sharp pain just below her abdomen. She knew she had trouble digesting certain foods, but she didn't take it seriously back then because she thought it was just a stomach bug. As she was trying to make sense of where that sharp pain came from, that's when she remembered her painful childhood memories. Particularly, she thought about the time when her family would constantly demean her and the kids at school would bully her. She would feel powerless and helpless in those moments. That's when she would feel harshly criticized and because she couldn't defend herself then, she would end up just swallowing her painful emotions. She was afraid that if she dared to protest or try to stop them, they would make her life even harder.

Now it all started to make sense. Rachel realized that all those emotions she suppressed for years were what was now affecting her so deeply. She knew that the tightness she felt in her stomach was signaling all the hurtful things she was made to feel, such as being made to feel like she wasn't good enough or good at anything. Thus, to avoid being seen as inadequate, Rachel coped by maintaining a pleasant persona and playing the role of the star child.

It all became too much as she started to feel like nothing she did was ever good enough. It seemed her family was rarely ever satisfied. That's when Rachel knew that her time to heal had come. She started using dance to express her emotions. Some days, she would find herself dancing along to loud and fierce rock music to release her unspoken anger and hurt. Other days, she would just scream and allow herself to feel her emotions without holding back any tears. After many times doing this, she soon started to feel lighter and was able to be more present in what she would be doing.

It was through diving into somatic awareness that Rachel was able to understand where her relentless drive to always be the best came from. Being anything less than the best meant to her that she would be seen as a failure and be treated poorly. Knowing she didn't want to ever feel invisible or small again, she decided to always try to do everything perfectly. But that approach to life was very unhealthy and unsustainable. She had trouble loving and accepting herself when she wasn't performing at her best. This would also make her very hard on others when they weren't doing things perfectly. She later learned that all that criticism she had in store for others was actually a reflection of how she treated herself.

The deep-seated core belief that was created in her during her traumatic childhood that she wasn't worthy unless she was perfect shaped Rachel's personality. She started taking on too much strain and overexerting herself to a point where her body tried to communicate with her through the recurring headaches and constant tightness.

She learned that the tension was actually her body's way of self-preserving and protecting her from the threats she felt (abandonment and rejection).

As she continued down the path of somatic awareness, she was able to lift off that heavy weight she carried and heal progressively. Her body and mind felt like they were in a beautiful harmonious dance once more. Her powerful story shows us the rewards that await us when we choose to honor our bodies by listening to the wisdom they have to share with us. I trust you too are now excited to see how somatic awareness can make your shadow work even more rewarding and fruitful.

To integrate somatic awareness in your everyday life and help your body process emotions better, remember to keep it active. Intentionally moving helps the body to start processing all that stored trauma and helps with lowering your cortisol levels too. That's why exercise is recommended for everyone, especially if they are struggling with any mental health challenges. The mere act of exercising gives your body more oxygen supply and helps to release tension and stress. It can also help you clear your mind. Below are some less strenuous activities you can try out:

- Tai chi
- meditative walking
- dancing
- qigong

- yoga
- Zumba
- stretching exercises
- belly breathing exercises
- martial arts
- aerobics
- jumping rope
- using the stairs instead of the elevator
- walking

Are you ready to support your mind-body connection more? I believe so! Let's say "goodbye" to our sedentary lifestyles and say "hello" to our enhanced active lifestyles where looking after our bodies daily takes top priority!

Chapter 7:

Embracing Self-Reflection to the Core

Whatever we don't reflect and perceive, we repeat. Have you noticed how we as humans often indulge in the same behaviors that keep us trapped in negative cycles until we finally reflect and gain insight into what's truly going on? However, although self-reflection holds the promise of gaining some enlightenment that can help us propel our lives forward, it's not always easy to do. Why? Let's see why through Rachel's story before her healing journey began.

The Power of Self-Reflection

Growing up in a family that was filled with chaos and intense emotional neglect, Rachel learned very quickly that the world wasn't a safe place. She learned not to depend on others. She also grew up feeling like a victim of her circumstances, almost powerless over the things that were happening in her life. She couldn't stop the echoing sounds of all the arguments she recalled her parents having while she was young. In a home where conditional love was the norm, she found herself constantly walking on eggshells, worried that she might make a wrong move and stir up more heated arguments in the family. Almost all her life, she felt pressured to be flawless. She tried her best to achieve this, which is why whenever someone pointed out her flaws, she would instantly feel triggered and become very defensive. She would blame others instead and fail to see how she could have also played a role in the problem that was there.

Although Rachel was a thinker by nature, it was still very hard for her to self-reflect objectively. Because she tried so hard to be perfect, all she desperately needed was people to validate her efforts and not only be quick to point out her flaws. This is what hardened her heart. The idea that people seemed to say very little when she did something right but the moment she did something wrong, it felt like, suddenly, all eyes were on her and people were eager to correct her. This upset her and made it hard for her to listen to feedback with an open mind.

Looking within objectively felt like self-betrayal because she felt like the world was against her, always ready to jump in and point out her mistakes. If she was to self-reflect, she thought that would be akin to joining the team of people tearing down her exhausted soul. She just didn't like it. She was already hard on herself. She felt terrified by the idea of having to face all the mistakes she made. Her wounds made her feel very insecure, so the thought of constantly looking there was awfully painful. Just being alone with her thoughts felt like opening a can of worms: unpleasant.

Due to her strong desire to be validated, her defensive attitude became stronger and stronger. She constantly felt the need to justify herself and prove herself because she felt like no one else cared to acknowledge how she felt. Her relationships became strained to a point where she failed to connect with her own family, friends, and partners deeply. Due to always feeling attacked, she became very closed off and would shut down during confrontational conversations. She didn't realize that her inability to pause, reflect, and accept responsibility for her actions made her come across as very selfish and inconsiderate to others.

She felt very misunderstood and drained. Every day was a battle with herself and the rest of the world. She kept explaining why she was the way she was by referring back to her childhood experiences. That's when one day, a friend who had heard her share the same story countless times eventually helped Rachel wake up to her senses. She lovingly showed Rachel how indeed what happened to her was wrong and certainly not her fault. But she was also able to show her a different perspective and remind her how, now, it's her responsibility to heal. That's when it dawned on Rachel that unless she pulls her sleeves up and starts to fully work on her healing and growth, nothing will ever change. She knew no one was coming to save her. She had to learn to be there for Rachel the right way before others could start showing up for her the right way.

Even though she didn't like writing, Rachel took it upon herself to start journaling after her meditation sessions. She learned that she didn't have to be afraid to look within if she was to explore what's happening from a place of love, not judgement.

Her way of dealing with feeling misunderstood used to be blocking people, walking away from inflammatory conversations, and keeping people at arm's length in her relationships. This somewhat made her feel justified because she felt like she was protecting herself from allowing people to hurt her. But the profound realization she had was that while on the surface it seemed like she was just avoiding toxic people, what she was truly running away from was her shadow self. She disliked how her traumas and fears had turned her into someone who was now timid, constantly on edge, and unable to build healthy relationships. Through self-reflection, she was now able to start noticing the painful emotions that were inside her; the fears, bitterness, unforgiveness, and hurt. She was also able to see the beauty that was radiating from her heart as seen through qualities she had like compassion, kindness, and resilience.

After discovering that she was running from her shadow for a good chunk of her life as she gazed deeply at her inner world, she could see that the emotions she was running away from were not there to hurt her. They all just wanted one thing: For her to listen to the messages they carried and decide to heal.

She stopped blaming others for how she felt. She was able to work on being her best self daily such that her relationships became enriched and harmonious. She no longer sees self-reflection as a bad practice of tearing herself down. Instead, she leveraged its transformative power.

Facing her shadow self helped her to notice many of the emotional blocks she had. In times when she would have reacted with outbursts of anger, she began to respond with more wisdom and clarity.

She saw how far she had come after noticing that before she embraced her healing journey, her life was a constant roller coaster ride of attracting toxic relationships with people who were also at her developmental stage. They too were stuck in painful cycles of avoidance, blame, self-hate, and defensiveness. She saw how all her relationships one way or the other seemed to mirror her hidden wounds and traumas. This would make her feel even more victimized. But as she became more enlightened, Rachel was able to start attracting people who mirrored her new level of maturity and healing.

Facing her shadow gave her so much insight into the emotional hurt that she had been carrying for so long. She had a hard time controlling her emotions when she was upset. She was also able to find out that all that was coming from her feeling hurt and not cared for the way she longed for. Instead of just reacting instantly, she trained herself to now take time to pause and come up with a more thoughtful response. Unpacking the unresolved emotions and pain helped her to no longer respond impulsively.

She achieved a sense of limitless joy and inner freedom and started to have more energy to inject into her passion projects. It felt so good to no longer be a victim of her past experiences. The radical transformation Rachel had was life-changing. She became a strong and healthy soul, ready to take on the world. That once seemingly daunting process of self-reflection made her open the doors she had long been waiting for... Doors of freedom, limitless love, and budding happiness.

Why We Run away From Self-Reflection

Can you sit still with yourself and your thoughts without having to find something to distract yourself with? Perhaps the idea of being alone terrifies you. Social media, doing all kinds of household tasks, and binge-watching Netflix can tend to be very tempting distractions. It seems like it's easier to just keep running and doing many things instead of pausing and properly checking whether we are headed in the right direction.

Why does it seem to be so hard to self-reflect? One reason could be that it takes up a lot of mental energy at times. So, mental and emotional fatigue do sometimes play a role. However, have you ever considered that some of the fatigue we feel comes from actually spending a lot of energy avoiding facing what we have to? You know, that emotional work we keep sidelining. Imagine how much energy it actually takes us to convince ourselves not to do something. Have you ever thought about how things in your life could work differently if only you decided to evaluate what's really been going on and learn from the past?

Another major reason why we avoid self-reflection tends to be our deep-seated need for comfort. Let's face it, the comfort zone can feel quite good. But all that pleasure is usually short-lived because we start to feel dissatisfied with where our lives are. Once we decide to leave our comfort zone, another fear strikes us; the fear of change. It can all feel so overwhelming having to deal with the uncertainty that comes with leaping in a new direction.

Our strong desire to be right can also hold us back from reflecting on ourselves and changing. We can start to feel very ashamed of admitting that we are wrong, and that's where the ego takes over. Our egos seldom want to admit that we are wrong; instead, they drive us to point outward and blame others for our problems and circumstances. However, doing that never makes things better; it's like giving away your power because once you think it's someone's fault, you won't take any responsibility for changing the situation. But when we look inward, we are able to take charge of the situation and correct what's wrong. Even if someone else was wrong, our willingness to admit to our faults and change them can also inspire others to change too.

Often, we have a certain way we perceive ourselves. For example, someone might believe that they are not selfish. They start to say that a lot and talk about how kind they are to others. But when others show them how their actions don't align with the image of themselves they have in their head, they can start to detest self-reflection. This is the essence of cognitive dissonance. It's when our actions are not in sync with our core values, so all that creates inner tension. Self-reflection becomes something that exposes that misalignment and makes us struggle to accept ourselves. Have you ever experienced this yourself?

In other cultures, self-reflection is at times viewed as a self-indulgent and vain thing. But we know that's not really true. Self-reflection is extremely important and the only way we can learn and grow. It’s a powerful practice that helps us connect with our higher self and let go of patterns that hold us back.

When done with a harsh and critical mindset, that's when self-reflection becomes destructive. Self-criticism can take root, leading us to spiraling down a dangerous path of dissecting our flaws to a point where we can hardly appreciate or see any beauty in ourselves. Often, reflecting on yourself this way only leaves you feeling defeated, drained, and even hopeless.

The goal of self-reflection should be to constructively self-reflect in a manner that's seasoned with grace a spirit of understanding, and love. If you were to self-reflect from this healthy perspective, what would that look like? How would you encourage yourself to grow without having to tear yourself down?

Constructive Self-Reflection

Do you have a mirror at home? What do you use it for? For noticing what's wrong so that you can fix it and look your best, right? Let's say you just finished bathing and are now combing your hair. How would you know if everything is perfectly in place? Through the mirror. Thus, mirrors play a pivotal role in our everyday lives. Without them, it would be impossible to know how we look and we would risk appearing inappropriate to the public. Through mirrors, we can know the kind of adjustments needed.

So, I have a question: When you want to use the mirror, do you ever run away or shy away from it? I bet you don't! Because you know that the mirror is your ally, not your enemy. Similarly, what would happen when you finally decide to have the same attitude towards your internal mirror? Instead of being afraid of it and avoiding it, see it as your friend there to help you look your best. This approach helps us harness self-reflection and see it as our friend who helps us illuminate our strengths and fix what blurs our shine. From now on, you can always decide to approach your writing with curiosity instead of fear.

Sometimes, we can be biased and find it hard to admit to ourselves things we need to change. That's why having a self-reflection partner can be so helpful. This is someone who can help us be accountable by holding up the mirror for us (objectively giving us constructive feedback). This should ideally be someone who love and cares about you. Someone you can trust to give you feedback on both your strengths and weaknesses. We all need that extra sets of eyes that can help us accelerate our growth. You can decide on the number of set times you will meet with that person to introspect on your lives and gain new valuable insights. What's crucial to remember about self-love is that the point of it is not to always pinpoint what's wrong. Instead, it is to embrace what's right, appreciate that, and grow into someone greater.

Self-Reflection Weekly Check-Ins: Suggested Questions to Use

Self-reflection shouldn't be something we just do when things hit rock bottom. Imagine how much we would grow if only we incorporated it as a non-negotiable part of our lifestyles. Making it a regular practice by setting aside time each day, week, and month to analyze what's been happening is pivotal. Doing this helps us uncover very important lessons about ourselves we need to know.

What can self-reflection look like as a daily practice? It could be you doing so every evening for just 10 to 15 minutes a day. You can learn what's working and what hasn't been working and then take some time to brainstorm ways you can make improvements to the areas you are evaluating.

Perhaps once a week you could also meet a loving friend (your accountability partner) and discuss how things have been. You could also journal together and check how your actions that week helped you move closer to your goals. Notice the areas you often slip and when fear takes the lead. Before finishing, make sure you have a clear way forward on how you're going to do things differently in the upcoming week. Doing this every week helps you to ensure that small obstacles don't end up becoming big problems that are harder to solve.

To help you get started with your self-reflection journey, consider trying out these prompts:

- What did I do really well this week?
- What did I learn from the hardships I faced this week?
- How did I regulate my emotions this week? Was I self-controlled? How did I lose my temper?
- What am I holding onto that's holding me back?
- Was I kind to myself this week?
- Which habits should I stop?
- Which new habits can I cultivate?
- Where do I lack empathy and compassion for others?
- Was I hard on myself at any point?
- Did I look after my mental health well?
- Which areas in my life do I need to develop more?
- Are there any fears holding me back?
- How do I present myself in my relationships?
- Is my conversation seasoned with grace and love?

- Am I still aligned with my goals? How can I invest more in achieving them?
- How can I live a more joyful life?
- Is there anything I'm avoiding? What am I afraid of?
- Am I growing as a person? Is my soul thriving?
- How can I be more authentic in my personal and professional life?

Remember that as you self-reflect, there will always be something new to fix and something new to celebrate. This means perfection is never the goal, but rather learning to enjoy the growth in the process. Think about it; we always find something new to fix on our faces when we look at the mirror. We don't let what we see make us sad or determine our mood for the day. Instead, we use what we see as constructive feedback to improve ourselves. Likewise, as you make time for self-reflection, always ensure that you also pause to take in and enjoy the good things you notice about yourself. But don't stop growing! Looking at your mirror with love and acceptance will help you to grow even quicker into a greater version of yourself.

Sometimes, you will experience moments of frustration and discomfort; that's totally okay. Embracing those times and checking what needs to be fixed will help you attain freedom and joy even quicker. You will find that most answers we are looking for are already within us. That's why our body and mind are just waiting for us to pause and think. Looking within gives us the keys to the life of freedom we are yearning for. Are you now excited to make self-reflection a fundamental part of your everyday life just as you look at your physical mirror every day? I believe you are! Let's keep moving forward.

Chapter 8:

Goal Setting for a Stellar New Beginning

Diving into shadow work can feel messy at times, but once you go through it all, there's only one outcome awaiting you: To emerge victorious at the end. The only way to see the light that awaits you at the end of the tunnel is to go through the tunnel and never stop until you catch it. Now imagine the feeling you will get once you know that you have broken free from the chains of your shadow that were holding you back. Just think about all the hope for a new beginning and the life with limitless possibilities that awaits you. Think about how enjoyable life will start to become once you're no longer constantly being dragged down by the weight of all the unresolved pain from your past.

I want you to take a moment to deeply think about it. Envision what your life will now look like each day as you move forward with a new approach. All those mistakes, shortcomings, and regrets that once weighed you down will cease to dictate your life as they Likewise, used to. Just imagine who you will become once those old limiting beliefs and stories that used to keep you small become powerless the more you embrace growth. What kind of person do you envision yourself becoming? What kind of life will you attract? How will you carry yourself and show up to the rest of the world each day?

When trauma takes the reins from us, we don't even realize how much we live most of our lives stuck in the past. So much of our energy is lost by focusing on either the past or the future. We end up failing to create the future we want because very little energy is being invested in the present. However, the goodness of shadow work is that you will no longer have to continue to live that way. Since you would have had time to process what happened in the past and how it affected you, it frees you to be able to start living in the present. And the more we do our best each day, the less worried we will have to be about our future.

That new beginning is right here. It's waiting for you to embrace it and believe that you deserve a different life that aligns with how awesome you are! With every season you will undergo, there's always something to enjoy and be grateful for. We will now jump onto that moving train headed to your true destiny and see how we can effectively set goals and prepare for a new beginning. Through being intentional, we will be able to not only dream about the lives we wish to have, but actually create a solid blueprint and plan of action regarding how that's going to be achieved. You aren't the type of person to live with dormant potential, no; you are the kind of person who believes in their capabilities and makes the most of every opportunity to become everything you are capable of being.

Let's get ready to dive into the goal setting work. As a beginner warm-up activity, I would like you to find a quiet and cozy place where you can envision your ideal future. Picture exactly how you want your life to be. Think about every aspect of your life. Which changes do you wish to see? When you travel right into that desired future with your mind, who do you see yourself as? Describe that person in as much detail as you can. Describe what that life will look like. That's going to be your blueprint and guideline for what you want to achieve. Where do you see yourself living? What kind of people will you be spending time with? What do you see yourself doing most of the time? Which hobbies do you see yourself enjoying? Financially, what exactly do you see yourself achieving? What is the common theme that's going to be prevalent in your relationships? All the answers you will write to these questions indicate exactly where your soul yearns to be. And, remember, whatever your soul or heart can conceive, you can certainly attain. Continue to brainstorm what that life will look like.

Once you're done, it will be time for us to turn that vision you just had into your reality. You have just decided who you want to be; are you now ready to put in the work that's required for you to get there? Let this new beginning be your heartfelt opportunity that you embrace with your all. Now it's time for you to rewrite the narrative and become everything your shadow self has been hoping you could be all these years.

Create a Vision Board

The first step for putting things into perspective is to gather materials for creating a vision board. You will need some scissors, magazines, a scrap book or nice board to write on, and different colored pens or a marker to write out any affirmations you want to stick on the board. Using pictures from a magazine is great because it gives you a visual of what you want to achieve which can get you excited whenever you look at those pictures. You need that excitement! Having that visual representation of all the things you want to achieve will also make it easier for you to remember your goals. Once you have written your vision board, place it somewhere you can look at every day. Even just one glance at it is enough to get that energy flowing and being pumped into chasing your dreams.

No more being defined by the past! No more being a prisoner to negative thoughts! Now you can create a beautiful life that aligns with your innermost dreams and desires. Any limitation that tries to reel you back to those old tales can be extinguished by the power of your positive affirmations and your remembering all you've already achieved so far. If you could do so much before, then what can possibly hold you back from achieving even greater things? Nothing! Believe this and watch that future you wrote on your vision unfold right before your eyes.

Reflect on What You Discovered During Your Shadow Work Journey

When we get an epiphany or very important insight in the moment, it's very easy to think that we will always vividly remember that lesson. But the brain doesn't actually work that way. Once the emotion you had in that moment wears down, it's easy to forget what was learned. So, make sure that take stock of all the lessons you learned so far. Write them down. Ensure they're engraved in your heart, but also somewhere you can always refer to; maybe your digital journal. Shadow work reveals to us so much about ourselves, so make sure you also write all you discovered about yourself through the process. Which hidden dreams, desires, strengths, and hopes did you realize you have through the process? Do you remember the limiting beliefs that used to keep you small and afraid to reach for more?

Using this insight you had, start to write new goals that reflect the real you that were always meant to be; that person your shadow was pushing you to become. Can you notice any new possibilities or attainable goals you can go after now that you know how to positively integrate your shadow into your everyday life?

Organizing your thoughts can be hard, but thankfully, there's an effective technique we can use to make the process even smoother for you. It's called the *SWOT Analysis*. Through this technique, you will be able to reflect on your Strengths, Weaknesses, Opportunities, and Threats respectively. Let's dive in and explore all these areas of your life.

Strengths

Think about things you are naturally good at. Maybe you're good at playing music, you have resilience in your character, or you keep your word, and so on. Write all those strengths you can think of. Your strengths will become the pillars you have in your life to support you when building that dream life you have in mind. Remember that doing your inner work helps you access the strengths of your shadow. That means it's highly likely that you already have these strengths:

- **Empathy:** Since you have empathy for your shadow, you will be able to exercise empathy for others too.
- **Assertiveness:** Since emotions like anger and aggression are often pushed to the shadow because of their reputation as

being bad things, doing your shadow work can help you access those emotions and express them in a healthy manner. The healthy version of these traits is known as *assertiveness*. You will now realize that when you integrate your shadow, you will have the courage to be bold and advocate for your well-being.

- **Self-Awareness:** Shadow work helps us to be self-aware, so it's highly likely that this is already one of your strengths.
- **Creativity:** All those repressed emotions you used to have or still have can help you tap into your potential. You can turn your story, fears, and untold secrets into inspirational work such as art or music that can also help others.
- **Resilience:** Chances are that you have already developed so much inner strength and endurance from having to carry a lot of weight on your shoulders without giving up. You can now use that resilience to overcome any obstacles that come your way in your journey ahead.

Weaknesses

What do you struggle with? Maybe you aren't a numbers person. Maybe you don't feel comfortable at social gatherings. Maybe you procrastinate and downplay yourself too much. Just take time to acknowledge any weaknesses you notice. Think about the feedback others have also given you on things you have to work on. If objective, that feedback can also help you understand your weak points better.

Opportunities

Which opportunities do you think are accessible now that you have done your inner work? How can you tap into your potential more and use your talents? Is there a new relationship or career prospects you can try out? How will you make the most of those opportunities?

Threats

Threats entail the challenges and obstacles you foresee coming your way. What will possibly limit you? What can jeopardize your growth and a new beginning? Maybe they're old habits you know often die hard. What do you think you can do once they start surfacing again? Knowing your threats in advance helps you to make a plan beforehand for how you will counter those challenges.

The SWOT Analysis gives you a strong foundation for self-introspection and setting your goals. It's like a road map that shows you where the nice terrain is and where the steep and rocky terrain is so that you won't have an accident and you can reach your destination on time safely.

Setting Authentic and Clear Goals Aligned With the Real You

The real you is your higher self that was obscured by all the unresolved trauma and pain from the past that was trapped in your shadow self. Remember that the goals you set back then used to reflect your level of development at that time. After doing inner work, we can't still set the same average goals anymore. The bar has to be raised high. Your goals have to reflect your new level of development and growth. That means dreaming big and believing that you are worthy of all that! The true superficial goals were your past goals that didn't match with your real potential. The ones you are setting now are goals that match your true status and worth. They should come from your heart; a heart that's now renewed and aligned with the truth of who you are.

Setting goals aligned with your authentic and higher self means having goals that reflect the truths your light and shadow were trying to tell you about yourself. They are the kind of goals that should show that every aspect of who you are deserves a place in this world and matters.

This means on this path, you will be able to achieve true self-actualization and fulfillment.

How to Set Goals

To get started, let's consider the timeliness with which you plan to achieve your goals. You can break them into the below categories to make the process much more effective.

- **Short-Term goals:** These are goals you can achieve within a month or a few. They can also connect to a larger goal you want to achieve long-term. Short-term goals can also be daily things you want to start doing such as waking up at 6 am every morning or exercising for one hour each day.

- **Medium-Term goals:** These are goals you typically want to achieve in 6-12 months' time. This is where you can add the new habits you wish to have established firmly in your daily routine, a new skill you want to learn, or new relationships you want to invest in.

- **Long-Term goals:** These are goals you would want to achieve in the long run (in years). They should reflect your bigger vision and dreams. Maybe it can be something like starting your own business, buying a new house, or getting a posh car. Your long-term goals should be big! Remember, you're going to grow so much every day, so you might also want to re-evaluate your goals from time to time to see if you have to adjust them so that they properly reflect your new growth each month.

Another standard framework you can use for setting goals is the famous SMART Goals criteria. That means setting goals that are:

- **Specific:** Name exactly what you want to attain. When you set vague goals, it leads to poor planning and vague results too.

- **Measurable:** Is there a way you can measure what success means to you? Perhaps you can consider putting an exact number if it's something you can put a numeric value to.

- **Attainable:** Considering your strengths, weaknesses, opportunities, and threats, what would a realistic goal look like?

- **Relevant:** Make sure that they are authentic and mean a lot to you. They should align with the person you are today.

- **Time-Bound:** To ensure that you don't end up losing time or procrastinating, set specific deadlines for when you want to achieve certain goals.

Kindness matters as you set your goals. The path to achieving them won't always be easy; some days will be good and others will be rough. But hitting an obstacle here and there doesn't mean that you're a failure. It just means you have to learn to always get up every time you're knocked down. That's what winning is truly about; getting up every time you fall and never giving up.

Preparing for Shadow-Based Obstacles

Remember that your shadow will still resist sometimes and try to inhibit your growth due to the fears and limitations that have been running through that part of you for years. From time to time, you might experience self-doubt or you might have a hard time beating the habit of being complacent. You may also still have a hard time admitting that you're wrong and find yourself getting defensive again.

When this happens, it's important that you remember that healing is a process. It takes time to break free from old habits, so give yourself some grace and compassion during that time. What matters most is getting right back on the right road if you find yourself veering off course. The only time you fail is if you choose to keep going down the wrong path. You can also use your moments of weakness as learning opportunities where you can discover more about yourself. Never equate losing to slipping into old habits. We all get tired sometimes or even forget what to do. And that's human. As long as you remind yourself what the right path is and commit to it again, you're winning!

Your Daily Life Should Bring Your Vision Closer to Realization

Goal setting is exciting and fun, but it can only work to our advantage when we make clear actionable steps we can take daily to achieve those goals. Every small, consistent step you take matters. All those steps accumulate to form that big dream you once had.

Start to prepare your days well in advance. Have time blocks for parts of your day when you will get certain things done and learn to value time more than ever before. Every night before you sleep, journal what you did that day to bring you close to your vision. Seek for new and better ways to achieve your goals. Don't be afraid to learn from others and ask for help. Reviewing how things are going creates a culture of feedback that helps you stay in check and aligned with your mission.

Sticking to your goals is truly a beautiful expression of true self-love. When we don't value ourselves, that's when we let other people and things come first. So, consider your commitment to achieving your vision as one of the deepest forms of self-love you will ever give yourself.

Chapter 9:

Thriving Through Relationships:

Opening Your Heart to Others

It's astounding to think of how impactful relationships can be. Think about it: What usually determines your answer when you describe your life? Often, we judge our lives through the kinds of relationships we have. Of course, other factors play a role like our finances and health, but ultimately, even those factors are influenced by how good we are at connecting and working with others. This shows the significant role relationships play in our lives. If the quality of our relationships is good, then we tend to feel more fulfilled. However, when things aren't looking good in our social lives, it can be very frustrating and stressful. That's why honing the skills of building strong relationships and sustaining them will be one of the best ways you can grow yourself.

Even though we already know that relationships matter, why do we sometimes shy away or avoid them? Maybe you also hear that internal voice that tells you that you're safer alone than with others. I bet we all feel this one at one point or another. We may view engaging with people as a very daunting and draining process, leading us to prefer solitude over having company. Avoiding socializing with others can make us feel very safe and make us think that we are more protected and less likely to get in trouble if we keep things on the low. However, as you may have already noticed, human beings truly aren't built for isolation. We thrive and feel joy when we are connected with others in meaningful ways.

If that's the case, if people have the ability to help us live happier and more developed lives, why is it that we still sometimes choose to live like islands? Why do we avoid or cut off connections that sometimes challenge us? Or even just avoid people altogether.

There are very understandable reasons why you may find yourself repeating that way of life. Let's now find out what they are and how we can have a paradigm shift to help us find a way to connect to others while also protecting ourselves from potentially harmful relationship dynamics.

Understanding Reasons Why We May Choose to Live Like Islands

Understanding reasons why we isolate ourselves at times should be done from a place of self-compassion and kindness. It's not so that we criticize ourselves, but that we use the mirror of self-reflection to help us become even better and grow. Most of the reasons we are about to uncover stem from childhood experiences, many of which you probably had little to no control over. Try to never blame yourself for having the relationship struggles and wounds you have. Instead, a more productive and progressive approach would be to understand what the wound is so that you can now know which remedy to use for it. By understanding your limitations or challenges, you will be a step closer to overcoming them and approaching your relationships with a fresher and healthier perspective. Let's now see what some of the main reasons for isolation tend to be; this also applies to anyone who has many people in their lives but chooses to keep them at arm's length.

Self-Preservation

Let's say you grew up being constantly let down and hurt by people you expected to receive love from, so your natural instinct became to avoid closeness. Why? Because in your mind, you will now be associating any form of closeness with pain. Instead of finding comfort in being close to someone, it can start to feel like a threat and even trigger you. Thus, in such cases, self-preservation becomes the coping mechanism that's employed to prevent yourself from being hurt again. This also can happen when you have been betrayed before, abused, misunderstood, judged, or abandoned before. Those adverse experiences from the past can start to shape how you perceive others. Even if someone didn't intend to hurt you, your body would still ring the fight or flight alarm system and feel threatened. That's why you might be distancing yourself from others in the hope that you won't keep reliving the same experiences.

Remember, even though it's possible that you can be hurt again, it's not entirely accurate that it means everyone will treat you that way. That means that isolation, while it might seem like a protective mechanism, might actually be holding you back from meeting and building relationships with wonderful people who can help you grow. Even those who don't treat us well still serve a good purpose if we choose to see things from a positive perspective. Through them, we can learn about areas we might have to work on; things that ordinarily people who care about you might struggle to openly share with you. But those who dislike you might be more direct about exposing your weaknesses. This means that even though it's intended to hurt you in this case, you don't have to allow them to win; you can still take the lessons you've learned and use them to your advantage.

Fear

This is where the "what ifs" dominate. Fear is a core emotion we all experience at one point or the other. Depending on our personality types and life experiences, we all find ourselves with different kinds of fears. Sometimes, you might even feel like you are afraid of everything. That's because fear is on a spectrum, so the degree to which we experience it for different things varies. For instance, you might have a strong fear of intimacy compared to your fear of being alone. We generally tend to feel afraid when we are vulnerable. We may ask ourselves, "What if they use what I'm telling them against me?" or "What if people reject me if they see my shadow side?" "What if people stop loving me once I try to get close to them?" All these kinds of fears are very real and in no way petty. They are real feelings that come from real concerns.

However, what's key to remember when we do experience these fears is that all of that is subjective. The only way we can know for sure if what we fear will happen is when we allow ourselves to go through what we are afraid of. In some cases, you may truly experience the outcome you dreaded. Although it may seem awful to go through that, it can also be a chance for you to grow and get to a point where you no longer worry about what people say or think about you. The other possible outcome that comes from walking through our fears and connecting with others anyway, even when we don't feel like it, is that we get a chance to realize that our fears might have all been just us overthinking things. Maybe reality isn't as harsh as you imagine it, but the only way to find out is to be intentional about doing whatever you can to be yourself and be your best. What happens after that, be it good or bad, is part of life. You can still walk away from that experience with your head held up high knowing that you did your best and didn't allow yourself to stay hiding because of your fears. You can be proud of that.

Emotional Overwhelm

If you're particularly a highly sensitive person or an empath, you probably noticed that it's easy for you to absorb other people's energies. Even if you aren't those things, we all sometimes feel drained after interacting with people. Or even the mere thought of being around others can feel very emotionally exhausting.

Social interactions require us to put our energy and time into them. If you've had a busy work day and many other adult responsibilities, socializing might be the least of your priorities. In such cases, it's also very normal to feel like you aren't up for having some company with you. Needing space is something you shouldn't have to feel bad about. It's a basic human need.

How would you say you normally feel after you spend time with people? Do they drain or energize you? Maybe some people do and some don't. To help us grow if we have been feeling depleted by others, we can consider taking a different approach. Instead of avoiding people completely, maybe you can plan your time in advance and allocate specific times for nourishing your relationships. This is another way of setting boundaries and ensuring that even though you connect with others, you can still be able to balance things. Effective boundary setting can help you not to lose yourself while you are connecting with others.

Need for Control and Perfection

If you were raised to always be the star kid and never make mistakes, you might feel the pressure to always be perfect around others. Just the thought of making a mistake can feel very daunting to you because you might be associating it with rejection and abandonment. Or maybe the idea of not being flawless makes you feel like you're not good enough or won't fit well with others. This belief that "I have to be flawless around others," is what can drive us into isolation because it's just altogether too much pressure. You might feel like people will judge you if you're not perfect or you might be humiliated. These imagined outcomes can get in the way of us seeing any positive thing that possibly comes out of connecting with others. The idea that maybe you have to always cater to people's feelings and say only the right thing can make social connections feel like too much work.

To help you grow from here, if you feel like this point resonates with you, consider thinking of people that you normally see thriving socially. Are they perfect people? Do they always say the right thing? Chances are that they aren't at all. But why is it that they seem to be socially accepted and loved? Usually, it's because those people often come from a place of strong self-acceptance. So, because they don't judge themselves or imagine the worst possible outcome happening, they naturally have people mirror the same energy of acceptance that they exude. The same way they don't punish themselves for their flaws or mistakes is the same way others also become more lenient and less concerned about their mistakes. What matters most is showing up as your authentic self and having confidence in that person no matter how many flaws the authentic version of you might have.

Trusting your worth and shining that light on others helps them see you from a positive perspective. Avoiding putting ourselves out there only gets in the way of growth and makes us miss out on so many opportunities. No one is perfect, so expecting perfection from yourself and others can only drive you further into isolation because no one will feel like they're good enough around you and with you. What matters most is connecting with others and learning when to say "no" when it's time to exert your limits.

Phobias (Social Anxiety)

What does the idea of walking into a room full of people make you feel like? Maybe you think about all the nerves that will start to kick in; the sweaty palms, the stuttering voice, the awkward moments. Envisioning all this before going to places with people can convince you not to go at all. What causes most of our phobias and fears is usually imagined scenarios we create in our own minds. That's why it's crucial to still challenge ourselves and test if what we think is really true before reinforcing that narrative.

Other phobias stem from traumatic experiences like being abused by someone or growing up in an unsafe environment. All these reasons are valid. However, staying in those fears and allowing them to confine you to a life without quality relationships can only end up hurting you even more than the original hurt you might have gone through. That's why it's crucial to still expose yourself, slowly but surely, to places where you can challenge your fears (Exposure Therapy). You don't necessarily have to make a huge social gesture, but just taking small, consistent steps each day and trying to reach out to others can help you progressively grow out of your fears.

Confidence often comes from the positive experiences we went through before. It's knowing that you once did well before that can give you the belief and strength to try again in the future because you know that success is attainable.

Overall, we've seen how at the core of isolation is the presence of fear. Maybe isolating yourself is your form of controlling your life experiences so that you don't end up going through the same unpleasant situations you may have experienced. However, as we've already discussed earlier, the only way to know if what you fear is real or imagined is to just allow yourself to go through experiences. Doing this will help you reshape your worldview and enable you to grow wiser and more socially skilled as well.

Why We Need Others to Help Us Become Our Best Selves

As human beings, *connection* is one of our core needs; it's really not something we can live without. It's an essential ingredient to a happy and healthy life. Just think about how bleak your life would be without fruitful and meaningful relationships. Doesn't just thinking of that life make you cringe or feel low?

Distancing ourselves from people does, at times, feel like a clever way to protect our hearts, but the reality is that it only deprives us the opportunities for growing and enjoying the benefits of meaningful connections. If we had wrong beliefs and ideas, that means we continue to have those ideas and beliefs for a long time because our hearts won't be open to hearing from other perspectives that can help us grow.

We are all created to co-exist together helping each other. Just think of what happens when predators are looking for prey. They often attack the vulnerable animal that's often weak and alone. That can also be us when we isolate ourselves, we become very vulnerable to the harsh realities of life when we don't have others to lean on in our times of need. We also need people to help us refine our characters so we can evolve into being our best selves. By interacting with others, we also get a chance to understand ourselves better as we get to see how we respond and react to different situations. When others reflect back on our weaknesses or strengths, it helps us know what to do to improve ourselves. Your relationships can become valuable mirrors that help you remove all that's blocking your beauty from shining.

When we only rely on our own thoughts, it leaves us growing at a very slow and stunted pace. We need others if we are to experience accelerated growth. Through people, we can receive the guidance and education we need in different areas. It can be anyone, whether it be your family, friends, mentors, a stranger, or just people you love. There's so much wisdom we can gain from hearing what they have to say and seeking help from them. We all have different nuggets of wisdom from the varied experiences we went through. Even though we may not all have the answers to all the questions we have, connecting with others helps us to put together all those suggestions and form a well of wisdom that we can always draw from.

Just think about all those times someone else's perspective helped you to grow or avoid getting into trouble. When we get to see how others navigate their lives and treat themselves, we can learn so much from them. Let's say you grew up in a family where you weren't emotionally validated or taken care of. Qualities like empathy and self-compassion might be very hard for you to master. But through connecting with people who are strong in those areas, you can watch how they do things and also start to mirror their behavior. By doing this, your soul is changed day by day. Just seeing how others treat themselves can also help us to love ourselves better. You can start to also hold space for your flaws and handle things differently based on all the social lessons you get to see.

How to Face Relationship Challenges and Not Run Away From Them

Do you secretly imagine having rosy relationships where it's all peace and no conflict or misunderstandings? We all dream of this and even believe it exists, especially after watching so many movies that depict one-sided stories. The reality of life is that every relationship comes with its own set of challenges. It can be shocking to feel like the very person who makes you happy is the same person who sometimes makes you feel very worthless or unloved. Even those we love can become sources of constant emotional distress and frustration.

When you do notice this pattern, what do you usually conclude? Do you think that those relationships weren't meant to be? What you will find interesting is that every relationship comes with its own problems. However, having problems doesn't mean it's a sign that you should now cut people off and conclude that they're bad for you. It's just a sign that we're all human and those challenges can be seen as opportunities for growth. Conflicts can feel very devastating and even traumatic. But how often have you noticed that after having a conflict, you may end up actually being closer to each other? Why? Because during conflicts people tend to tell each other the truth and express their suppressed needs more. That's why a deeper connection is created. However, as you mature, you will notice that you don't always have to fight to express your needs or get what you want. There are other ways to express what you want cordially and harmoniously.

The key to having successful relationships is learning to have realistic expectations for yourself and others. The next step would be learning how to communicate those expectations in a way that's palatable to the other person.

The goal of relationships is not to always have things done perfectly all the time. Rather, it's to grow with each other daily and help bring out the best in one another. Imagine what would happen if you no longer door-slam people and start inviting them into your life to face your differences together and sort things out harmoniously. How many friends would you have? How many close relations would you have with your family members? Sometimes, avoiding people might feel like a strength when we make ourselves believe that we are protecting ourselves, but deep down, I'm sure you and I already know that avoidance usually comes from a place of fear.

Now, what if you decide to start shifting things and being more willing to work through problems by seeing them as opportunities for growth and more fulfilling connections? What would happen? How would your social dynamics work out if you decide to move in that direction going forward?

What often makes things very difficult in relationships is that we may be very unaware of our shortcomings. So, when they get shown to us, it can become very triggering. It can provoke us to anger and this then boils down to having full-blown arguments or avoiding each other. That's why it's crucial to invest in becoming more self-aware. Reading books helps, but what's even more effective is exposure therapy. This means that you now have to be intentional about exposing yourself to relationships and being vulnerable. By showing up as your authentic self, you can get feedback from others on things you may have to change or be aware of. Once you're aware of how you operate, it becomes easier to break free from negative patterns that make it hard for you to have thriving relationships.

Close your eyes now and think of a recurring problem that comes up in your relationships. If you were to stop blaming others, how would that problem be solved? What can you do to correct the part you played in creating that problem? Remember, what makes looking inward effective is that through being self-aware, you can empower yourself to start making positive changes that will impact your experiences.

Communication is extremely important when it comes to relationships, but is it always easy to have effective communication? Often, it's not. It can take time to know how to communicate in a way that the other person is able to comprehend and respond positively to. Successful relationships can happen whenever we decide to use wise approaches in dealing with issues that arise.

Knowing how to *repair the relationship and trust after a conflict* has occurred is also crucial for maintaining lasting relationships. When you hurt others, don't forget to take ownership and apologize sincerely. Changed behavior reaffirms to others your commitment to protecting the relationships you have with them. What do you think are some key actions that can help you take action to rebuild trust when it's broken?

Without empathy and consideration, it becomes very difficult to keep the trust strong. However, when we practice those qualities consistently, it helps the other person to feel loved and validated in the relationship.

By applying these relationship skills and a new mindset, you will be able to start breaking down the walls you may have built. What awaits you outside the life of isolation is limitless possibilities of thriving relationships and a holistically successful life. You deserve that life, so are you ready to go for it?

Chapter 10:

Leveraging Mindfulness and Grounding Techniques to Stay Connected to Your Truth

You know that moment when you feel like you are alive but not really living? I found that's what often happens when we live lives disassociated from our truth. Imagine what it would be like when you start being fully present with yourself each day. When you start allowing others to meet and connect with the real you... Life starts to feel different! Embracing authentic living is something we can achieve through harnessing mindfulness every day of our lives.

But after living so many years disconnected from ourselves and also trying to measure up to societal expectations, it can feel difficult to suddenly switch and step into your authentic self. But what's hopeful and empowering is knowing that it is possible. Just as you weren't born the way you are now but grew into developing the habits you have, you can also grow out of your current undesirable habits and master new ones with time, careful preparation, and execution.

Through this chapter, we will explore how you can use mindfulness as your best friend in helping you connect to your best self every day. We also look at some effective grounding techniques you can use to stay rooted in your truth and live a life aligned with your new core values and a renewed sense of self.

The Power of Mindfulness

The word mindfulness now seems to be a buzzword. And often when something becomes a buzzword, we can get too familiar with it and lose touch with how powerful it is or take it for granted. Mindfulness happens to be one of those things that can help you to make the most of your opportunities and actively create the life you want. It's one thing to dream, but it takes a lot of mindfulness to be able to recognize when it's time to work hard for those dreams and not let any opportunity pass us by.

But what is it really? Mindfulness is mastering the art of being present. Often, we repeat the same old behavioral cycles and thoughts because of not being fully aware of what's happening. But what if we could pause and quiet down all those buzzing thoughts in our heads that are often visiting the future of the past? What would happen when we are fully present and choose to concentrate our energy on one important thing at a time? Mindfulness is that skill that will help you to truly experience each hour of your life and actively participate in creating the future you want by being present and dedicated to being your best today and tomorrow.

What makes mindfulness special is that through practice, you're able to grow your level of self-awareness. You also become more aware of what's happening around you. Have you ever spoken to someone and felt like you're talking to yourself? Maybe their body language gave you signals that indicated that they weren't truly there. Or maybe they just couldn't remember what you were saying and their energy seemed off. All such things remind us of how mindfulness can be impactful, even in our daily interactions. Without it, those we engage with may not feel heard or seen. But now imagine what would happen when you are fully present when engaging with others? Quality conversations and relationships! All because you managed to fully bring your whole self to that present moment.

Thus, we can see that mindfulness is that vital bridge that will help us leave our imaginary worlds and allow us to actively connect with reality and action out our plans. But how do we develop such an awesome skill in a world where there's just so much noise and countless things to worry about as adults?

The answer lies in learning to pay attention to our thoughts, what's going on around us, how we feel, and even being aware of past experiences. Mindfulness is achieved by intentionally paying attention to what's going on in your world without judgment. Through this practice, you can relieve your brain from being overwhelmed with all sorts of worries and just train it to focus on what needs to be done, step by step. As you fully apply yourself to what's going on in your present moment, you will start noticing that you will no longer have to continue to play catch-up with life. Things no longer happen without you noticing them. You become very aware of what's happening which empowers you to move forward in the best direction available using all the information you would have observed and learned.

Living this way requires us to start practicing emotional and mental discipline. Through mindfulness, we are able to create space in our minds for processing the present and living fully, one day at a time. It allows us to also start to breathe and enjoy the beauty of our lives.

Through mindfulness, you will begin to start noticing things more. All that's required is that you practice bringing your full senses to what's happening in your present moment. Even something as simple as being aware of your breathing pattern, how nice it feels to walk on a smooth carpet, or just gazing intently at someone is all part of mindfulness. It opens your eyes to seeing and appreciating life as it is.

Benefits of Mindfulness

Beyond helping us to be present, mindfulness also comes with many other advantages. Let's explore some of its key benefits:

- **Stress and Anxiety Reduction:** Have you noticed that it's usually our fears, worries, and thoughts that make us troubled and anxious? Sometimes, this goes on to the point where we are afraid of things that haven't even happened yet or might never happen. Sometimes, it's our thoughts that hold us back and keep us captive to our past mistakes and regrets. Even though you may have grown and are now a different person, negative thoughts can still come and try to stress you out and drag you back to where you used to be. Thankfully, through mindfulness, you will be able to tame all that madness. You will be able to discipline your thoughts and clear the mental chatter that doesn't propel you forward. All this will happen because your mind will be focused on the present which usually doesn't have as much drama as the past. What's mainly present in the now is just life as it is and countless opportunities waiting for you to dive into. Noticing the beauty of what lies in the present is what will also help to clear the stress and anxiety.

- **More Productivity:** Imagine what happens after all the mental chatter that often stresses us out quiets down? You will have so much more energy left for you to use for action. Instead of having decision fatigue and burning more energy by overthinking or worrying, all that time and energy can now be used for getting more things done.

- **Better Decision-Making Ability:** When we aren't aware of the entirety of what's going on, it's very easy to fall into poor decision-making. Through mindfulness, you will acquire more information from what you observe which allows you to make more informed and excellent choices. Your judgment also becomes better. Instead of making decisions based on assumptions or impulsivity, you will start to respond from a place of understanding rather than reacting from a place of fear or panic.

Mindfulness and Shadow Work

Our shadows only wreak havoc in our lives when we aren't aware of what's going on. Now that you've done your shadow work and are ready to make everything work to your advantage, nothing can stop your success. Through mindfulness, you will be able to start embracing all parts of yourself and giving more compassion and love to parts you used to harshly judge. You will also start breaking free from old behavioral patterns that may have caused you pain. Each day, you can start integrating your shadow. Instead of seeing your shadow traits as problems or something to be ashamed of, you will become to start seeing them as opportunities for growth through mindfulness. That shift that's needed for you to start loving and being kind to yourself and others will all happen through the power of mindfulness. Since we may have lived years being unkind to ourselves, it won't naturally come easy to suddenly start treating ourselves differently. However, through mindfulness, we can cultivate the habit of deeply loving ourselves with time until it becomes ingrained in our core nature.

Grounding Yourself in Your Truth

Let's think about this briefly. Each day, how often would you say you catch yourself desperately seeking validation outside? With the prevalence of social media, it can become a strong addiction to constantly measure our worth using what others think of us. But we found out that living that way isn't healthy or sustainable. People's opinions change all the time, which means if we base our worth on what they think of us, our sense of worth will always be shifting and unpredictable. But what if you can start using mindfulness to change that dynamic? Imagine how nice it must be to have a solid sense of self that doesn't shift, no matter what others think of you or what you acquire externally. That means you would have achieved what being truly grounded is all about. Relying on the noise outside to decipher who we are can veer us away from our truth about how inherently worthy we already are! To be grounded means now we have to embrace lives that are aligned with our core values and authentic selves.

What It Means to Disassociate From the Truth

Whenever we distance ourselves or live separate lives from our authentic truth, that's disassociation happening. This happens all the time when we try to shrink ourselves in order to fit into some social group or be accepted by others. It's when you abandon your true values, needs, feelings, and beliefs just to avoid discomfort or gain validation from others. Doing this for long is what leads to a life where one starts to feel very empty, unfulfilled, or like they can't even relate with themselves. Would you say you've ever felt this way? It's really not a nice feeling, right? No one deserves to continue to live that way. Part of loving ourselves deeply is learning to break away from any disassociation habits we have. This can be achieved through mindfulness, and the outcome is that you become a very grounded person.

The Role of Your Core Values

Another place you can start to look at when connecting with your truth is to know your core values well. If you aren't sure, you can come up with core values that reflect the kind of person you want to be. Core values are things you strongly believe in and stand for. Being one with your core values is another way you can start grounding yourself.

You can create your core values list by thinking about qualities that make you feel alive and truly authentic. For instance, honesty, kindness, respect. Write down everything you want to be known for. Then as you journey through your life each day, check in to see how your actions align with those core values. It's also your responsibility to educate people through your interactions. Have five main core values that will become the guiding principles in your life that you adhere to. Loving yourself deeply also means always advocating for those core values to be respected in your life. For instance, if your core value is respect, that means if someone disrespects you, you no longer allow them to get away with it. Instead, you lovingly guide them and help them to understand how best they can interact with you in order for the relationship to last. If they refuse to listen, then your responsibility would be to draw boundaries and not allow them to continue to treat you like that. This is also how we become grounded in our true personalities and let others see and connect with us for who we truly are.

Below are powerful affirmations that can help you to be grounded in your truth whenever you need positive reinforcement and a sense of direction (Jordan, 2022).

20 Affirmations for Staying Grounded and Authentic

1. Each day, I'm learning to trust myself more and more.
2. My feelings matter, and I make time to understand them.
3. I was born unique, and I am good enough.
4. I choose to stick to authenticity.
5. My worth is not defined by others.
6. Every part of me deserves to be loved and understood.
7. My values deserve my full respect. I align with them as much as I can.
8. I deserve to take up my space in this world and be seen for who I truly am.
9. I give myself the love I deeply yearn for.
10. Every day, I am changing into the best version of myself.
11. I choose to stay connected to the present where my true power resides.
12. My shadow is a part of me that has a voice I choose to listen to.
13. I embrace each opportunity to show my true self.
14. I choose to no longer judge myself or others but extend compassion instead.
15. I embrace taking worthwhile risks and living a bold and big life.

16. My truth stands, even when the winds are blowing. I choose to stick to it.

17. Every day is an opportunity to lavish myself with love.

18. I choose to be generous with my spirit.

19. My voice will be heard.

20. My life is a gift I choose to embrace with a heart of gratitude and courage each day.

When our lives aren't taking the forms we wish for them to take, our default thinking might be to assume that the solution is outside our control, but that's not true at all. As we've seen, within us lies so much potential waiting for us to dive into and unleash. Remember that vision board you made? Now the time has come for you to create that life. It's going to be possible because we will only focus on being present and not worrying about yesterday or tomorrow anymore. The goal is to be consistent in doing what needs to be done, one day at a time. Over time, all those small daily wins will turn into a life of victory that you will love. Are you ready to start rebuilding your life with your renewed wisdom and determination? What lies ahead of you is only triumphant if you choose to remain true to yourself and put in the necessary work. It will be incredible to start seeing all your relationships change drastically as you begin to shower yourself with all that love you used to wait for others to give you. Guess what? You did it! You embraced your shadow work journey already just by learning about it.

Conclusion

Throughout this book, we've seen how the power of living deeply fulfilling lives lies in our hands. Moving forward, we can start working on our visions and creating the lives we dearly long for.

Shadow work might feel a bit messy at the start as you learn to face your painful and uncomfortable emotions, but just look at how far you've come now! You were able to push through all the discomfort and reach out your hand to your true self who was desperately crying out for your love and attention.

It makes sense why it's so hard to love ourselves when we aren't true to who we are. It's because it's not us! What we deeply desire is to connect to our true identity and shine the light of who that person is onto the world. Now you get the chance to redesign your life and declutter all that doesn't have to remain there anymore.

What's even more special than having a big and beautiful house to live in is to make our hearts those beautiful homes. It's learning to love and care for our minds, hearts, and bodies in such a way that shows that we understand that that's where we will live for the rest of our lives. If our mind, heart, and body follow us for the rest of our lives, then isn't it true that there's nothing that should matter more than looking after all of who you are? Friends come and go, jobs come and go, but you will always have you. Thus, the journey you took to invest in yourself and heal through shadow work is one of the best gifts anyone can ever give themselves. For that, I would like to thank you.

Thank you for already loving yourself enough to invest in growing and starting a new life that reflects who you truly are and what you stand for. Thank you for loving yourself deeply. You might not think you do, but the fact that you're here and you're doing this for yourself speaks for itself.

I can't wait to hear more about your growth journey as you continue to embody your truth in its entirety. If you're inspired to leave a review on Amazon, I would be delighted to read it. I'm certain that your sharing your journey with other readers and how you found this book will also encourage them to dive into the beauty of shadow work. May your path ahead be filled with limitless love, joy, and amazing opportunities. Well done, once again. You really did it!

About the Author

Maria Sage Starling is a dedicated writer and passionate advocate for personal growth and self-discovery. She lives in the vibrant city of New York with her children and dog. Maria brings a unique blend of life experience and empathy to her writing. As a middle-aged woman who has faced significant personal challenges, including health issues, life transitions, and moments of profound loss, she understands the journey of re-discovering oneself in adversity. Her experiences have deepened her commitment to self-development and have fueled her passion for helping others navigate their own paths to healing and empowerment.

Maria's writing is deeply rooted in her belief that every challenge presents an opportunity for growth and that authentic living requires embracing all facets of oneself. Her books reflect this philosophy, offering practical guidance and compassionate support to those looking to improve their lives, deepen their relationships, and nurture their families. With a focus on mindfulness, emotional Intelligence, and effective communication. Maria provides readers with tools to enhance their personal and family lives.

When not writing, Maria enjoys walking her dog, cooking, traveling, and spending time in nature. She is passionate about helping others find balance, purpose, and joy. She believes that every challenge is an opportunity for growth and transformation. Her work is a phenomenal reflection and reminder of the limitless potential for personal renewal every human inherently has.

References

Ackerman, C. E. (2019, July 10). *Twenty three amazing health benefits of mindfulness for body and brain.* PositivePsychology.com. https://positivepsychology.com/benefits-of-mindfulness/

Applegate, D. (2023, March 26). *Shadow work and self-discovery: Overcoming common obstacles.* Rediscovering Sacredness | Dominica Applegate. https://rediscoveringsacredness.com/shadow-work-self-discovery-overcoming-common-obstacles/

Being, G. (2024, March 7). *Shadow work exercises for personal & spiritual growth.* Grace Being. https://grace-being.com/carl-jung/shadow-work-exercises/

Chelsie. (2022, August 15). *Fun ways to connect with your inner child.* Relationship Enrichment Center. https://www.relationshipenrichmentcenter.com/blog/2022/fun-ways-to-connect-with-your-inner-child

Crawford, S. R. (2019, August 23). *People are mirrors.* Medium. https://medium.com/@authorsrcrawford/people-are-mirrors-94cd92da4fed

Deanna. (2022, May 26). *Journal prompts for when you feel totally out of control* . Life by Deanna ›. https://lifebydeanna.com/journal-prompts-for-when-you-feel-totally-out-of-control/

Eash J. (2023, October 8). *How to practice mindfulness with shadow work.* Medium. https://medium.com/@readingwitheash/how-to-practice-mindfulness-with-shadow-work-565ae3a07813

Garnermann, J. (2017). *The origin of the shadow.* Jung Centre. https://www.jungcentre.com/the-origin-of-the-shadow

Griffiths, N. (2022, May 3). *Forty shadow work prompts for self-Love.* Seeking Serotonin. https://seekingserotonin.com/shadow-work-for-self-love/

Hoy, C. (2022, September 29). *The ultimate guide to making productive weekly check-ins.* Www.joinassembly.com. https://www.joinassembly.com/blog/how-to-make-weekly-check-ins-productive

Innertune Content Team. (2023, November 11). *Hundred love affirmations for strong relationships.* Innertune Blog What You Think, You Become.; Innertune Blog What You Think, You Become. https://blog.innertune.com/love-affirmations-for-relationships/

Ishler, J. (2021, September 16). *How to release "Emotional baggage" and the tension that goes with it.* Healthline; Healthline Media. https://www.healthline.com/health/mind-body/how-to-release-emotional-baggage-and-the-tension-that-goes-with-it#where-emotions-are-stored

Jordan. (2022, May 11). *Thirty one strong affirmations for grounding.* Spirited Earthling. https://www.spiritedearthling.com/affirmations/31-strong-affirmations-for-grounding

Kelsay, A. (2023, June 14). *Practicing somatic or body awareness* . Progress Counseling - Portland, Oregon. https://progresscounselingllc.com/practicing-somatic-or-body-awareness/

Leonard, K., & Watts, R. (2024). *The ultimateguide to S.M.A.R.T. goals.* Forbes Advisor; Forbes. https://www.forbes.com/advisor/business/smart-goals/

Lewis, J. (2023, May 25). *Exploring your shadow self: 30-day shadow work prompts to deepen your self-awareness.* Www.zellalife.com. https://www.zellalife.com/blog/exploring-your-shadow-self-30-day-shadow-work-prompts-to-deepen-your-self-awareness/

Mayer, B. A. (2021, July 27). *Do you have a dark side? Shadow work experts say yes.* Healthline. https://www.healthline.com/health/mental-health/shadow-work#exercises

Melillo, A. (2020, February 18). *Healing + Releasing emotional shadows.* Ashley Melillo. https://www.ashleymelillo.com/blog/healing-releasing-emotional-shadows

Morsner, R. (2023). *When does self-reflection become self-destructive.* Odyssey Magazine. https://odysseymagazine.co.za/when-does-self-reflection-become-self-destructive/

Patek, A. (2021, January 25). *Bringing the shadows to light: Reparenting yourself in motherhood.* Genmindful.com; Generation Mindful. https://genmindful.com/blogs/mindful-moments/bringing-the-shadows-to-light-how-motherhood-helped-a-mom-heal-from-trauma

Perry, C. (2015, August 12). *The Shadow.* Society of Analytical Psychology. https://www.thesap.org.uk/articles-on-jungian-psychology-2/about-analysis-and-therapy/the-shadow/

Seligman, C. (2020, May 28). *How shadow work can lead to deeper self-love: A simple way to begin – PsychoSocial.* Psychosocial.media. https://psychosocial.media/2020/05/28/how-shadow-work-can-lead-to-deeper-self-love-a-simple-way-to-begin/

Shaffar, D. H. (2015, March 17). *Reconnecting with your inner child - Visualize your way to healing - Alpha Center for Divorce Mediation.* Alpha Center for Divorce Mediation. https://www.alpha-divorce.com/children-and-divorce/inner-child-visualization/

Staff, S. (2022, January 26). *Practicing mirror work for self-love: The 8-Step Guide.* SOLANCHA. https://solancha.com/practicing-mirror-work-for-self-love-the-8-step-guide/

Taets, J. (2024, August 12). Self-reflection as a superpower. *Forbes.* https://www.forbes.com/councils/forbesbusinesscouncil/2024/01/30/self-reflection-as-a-superpower/

Teule, E. (2015, March 10). *Reclaiming the gifts of your inner child.* Ekhart Yoga. https://www.ekhartyoga.com/articles/wellbeing/reclaiming-the-gifts-of-your-inner-child

Toni-Anne. (2022, November 10). *Shadow work & somatics* . Medium; Medium. https://medium.com/@contact_3087/shadow-work-somatics-5114b8952d04

Vayner, M. (2020, October 29). *Discover the transformative magic of shadow work.* Misha Vayner - Your Well Guide. Misha Is a Trauma Informed Holistic Health and Life Coach.; Misha Vayner. https://mishavayner.com/shadow-work/

Vrlak, A. (2023, March 4). *Body scan meditation: A complete guide.* Mindfulness Exercises. https://mindfulnessexercises.com/meditation/body-scan/

Weingus, L. (2022, May 17). *Forty-five journaling prompts to help heal your inner child and unleash joy.* Silk + Sonder; Silk + Sonder. https://www.silkandsonder.com/blogs/news/inner-child-journal-prompts?

Williams, P. (2023, March 15). *An open letter to my inner child - The Conscious Way - Medium.* Medium; The Conscious Way. https://medium.com/the-conscious-way/an-open-letter-to-my-inner-child-5c97a0bf088e

Williamsburg Therapy Group. (2024, March 20). *Why do people isolate themselves?* Williamsburgtherapygroup.com; Williamsburg Therapy Group. https://williamsburgtherapygroup.com/blog/why-do-people-isolate-themselves#

Wright, J., & 2022. (2022, January 16). *Thirty shadow work prompts for healing and growth.* PureWow. https://www.purewow.com/wellness/shadow-work-prompts

Made in United States
North Haven, CT
12 May 2025